ANGEL
First Aid

Remedies for Life, Love, and Prosperity

SUE STORM
"The Angel Lady"

STERLING ETHOS
An imprint of Sterling Publishing Co., Inc.

New York / London
www.sterlingpublishing.com

STERLING and the distinctive Sterling logo are registered trademarks of
Sterling Publishing Co., Inc.

Library of Congress Cataloging-in-Publication Data

Storm, Sue.
  Angel first aid : remedies for life, love, and prosperity / Sue Storm.
    p. cm.
  Includes index.
  ISBN 978-1-4027-7087-6 (alk. paper)
  1. Angels. I. Title.
  BL477.S76 2010
  235'.3--dc22

                                        2009027654

10 9 8 7 6 5 4 3 2 1

Published by Sterling Publishing Co., Inc.
387 Park Avenue South, New York, NY 10016
© 2010 by Sue Storm
Distributed in Canada by Sterling Publishing
$^{C}/o$ Canadian Manda Group, 165 Dufferin Street
Toronto, Ontario, Canada M6K 3H6
Distributed in the United Kingdom by GMC Distribution Services
Castle Place, 166 High Street, Lewes, East Sussex, England BN7 1XU
Distributed in Australia by Capricorn Link (Australia) Pty. Ltd.
P.O. Box 704, Windsor, NSW 2756, Australia

Manufactured in the United States of America
All rights reserved

Sterling ISBN 978-1-4027-7087-6

For information about custom editions, special sales, premium and
corporate purchases, please contact Sterling Special Sales
Department at 800-805-5489 or specialsales@sterlingpublishing.com.

Illustrations on pages iv, 3, 9, 159 copyright © 2010 Robin Williams

With fond memories of my dear mother, Anita Belkin, whose love of writing has led me to the same path. My mother encouraged the development of my "special gifts," and I am extremely grateful for her wisdom in this area. Thank you, Mom, for your loving support.

Message from Archangel Michael

Angel First Aid provides guidance to people who are looking for understanding and prosperity in their lives. The Guardian Angels offer the insight that leads to happiness and abundance in every aspect of life.

Contents

Acknowledgments

Writing *Angel First Aid* was a labor of love for me and my talented "Angel Assistants," Kathy Hulina, Monica Lee, and Joan Sweeney.

Others contributing included Tom Hulina, Allison Brewster, Sharell Jordan, Mel Sipiora, Vickie Farina, Norma Watts, and Mel Dean.

Acknowledgment is being given to my daughter, Rochelle Storm, who is always available for her superb encouragement and support.

Recognition is offered to my family: Major Belkin, Hannah Storm, Mel Dean, and the Belkins: Joan and Steven and Tikva and Bernie.

Gratitude, along with special thanks, to my agent, Stephanie Tade. Her faith in Guardian Angels and *Angel First Aid* is heartwarming.

Appreciation is extended to my terrific mentors: Darla Engelmann, Genevieve Paulson, and Linda Howe, for their gift of insight.

Acknowledgment and appreciation to God, "My Little Man," and the angels, for *Angel First Aid* is truly the product of their creation.

The Angel Lady

My original encounter with angelic intervention took place in East Grand Rapids, Michigan. At eighteen months of age, tangled up in my blankets and suffocating, I had a near-death experience. I saw several angels flying over my head. Somehow, these angels alerted my mother, relayed information about my dilemma, and made it possible for me to be saved. Then, on my fourth birthday, I heard a special male voice that offered guidance. I affectionately named the voice "My Little Man." He gave me advice, described future events, and taught me to visualize what I desired. As a child, I received tools for success.

Fast-forward thirty years. I went to the University of Michigan, married, and was raising my daughter. After moving to Illinois, an extraordinary event transpired that would change the course of my life. One night, while I was at work in the warehouse of my bowling supply distributorship, the ceiling appeared to open up, and a loud, booming voice called out: "Sue, you have to help people!" My body seemed to tremble as I resonated with the power of this command. I responded immediately: "Yes, God, what do you want me to do?" His answer came later, as I found that I could fulfill God's directive to "help people" through consulting and speaking about love, happiness, and prosperity.

In 1996, My Little Man said, "Make a writing room." Little did I know that the angels had a plan. This room was being readied for authors Barbara Mark and Trudy Griswold to edit a second book. While we were collaborating, these extraordinary women revealed that My Little Man was actually Archangel Michael! He has guided me toward my purpose in life. My path has led me to a life centered around consulting on angelic communication.

1

Angels Among Us

Angels are true messengers of God and were specifically created to provide guidance, advice, and protection. Monotheistic religions throughout the world recognize and report the existence of angels. History has portrayed angels in writings, symbols, and teachings. Most religions, including Christianity, Judaism, Islam, and other spiritual traditions, acknowledge the angels as God's messengers. While angels are recognized in all religions, it is not necessary to have a specific affiliation to receive blessings.

Four significant and powerful celestial beings that are known as Archangels tend to humanity. They provide assistance to large numbers of individuals and can be found handling a broad range of duties and responsibilities. Guidance and protection are major ones. Ever-present, they have boundless energy and are ready for intervention whenever they are summoned.

Guardian Angels work with individuals to identify and pursue their purposes in life. They offer guidance in finding appropriate careers and professional opportunities. Selected for individuals at birth, the Guardian Angels bestow multiple blessings of happiness and prosperity. An assignment for them is to render care, love, and guidance to all living beings.

Angel Specialists are Guardian Angels who have expert status in a particular area. People benefit from knowing what facet of life an Angel Specialist handles. Individuals can then choose the exact Specialist best suited for the circumstance or situation. Sometimes angels assume human form for a period of time to serve a specific purpose. Referred to as "Physical Angels," they appear, perform an assigned task, and then immediately depart.

People who have passed away can take on the form of an angel and return intermittently to the Earth plane. Their arrival can often be evidenced by a unique sign or symbol, a familiar fragrance, an appearance in a dream, or the movement of a recognizable object. Leaving the Earth once their assignment has been completed, they will reappear as circumstances warrant.

Archangels and Guardian Angels can be instantly dispatched. They come to Earth either in larger groups or independently, to be of assistance to humanity. Angels are ready to provide guidance to those who wish to improve the environment and to advance world peace. There is no limit to what angels can do!

How to Use This Book

Angel First Aid is your guide to connecting with angels who offer sincere love, guidance, and support. This book demonstrates how to make your life happier and more prosperous by teaching you to reap the benefits of angelic knowledge and wisdom. You will learn to use *Angel First Aid* as a guidebook and a means of approaching life with a fresh and positive perspective.

This book presents practical suggestions for finding happiness and fulfillment. Topics covered correlate with the angels' definition of prosperity: success in every aspect of life! Included are tools for attaining good health, greater happiness, and financial well-being. Angels offer sound advice on how to make life easier, simpler, and profitable for you and your family.

Angel First Aid is filled with activities and visualizations. The book contains remedies designed to enhance physical, emotional, mental, and spiritual well-being. These remedies are also known as Angel First Aid Techniques. They become tools to enrich your life. Using *Angel First Aid* as an everyday reference will be enormously effective. The benefits are cumulative, generating the power to help you enjoy a more prosperous lifestyle.

Perform the Angel First Aid Techniques and gain the positive results. Regard the remedies as recipes from an angelic cookbook. All the exercises can be used individually, or they can be combined. When practiced regularly, these techniques become valuable tools for achieving happiness and success.

How This Book Is Organized

Miracle Stories are narratives from individuals who have had their lives dramatically changed after experiencing extraordinary events involving Guardian Angels. Every amazing story reveals how these encounters have left a profound impact on all those who have been touched by the benevolence of angels.

The twelve chapters feature the following components:

Affirmations—declarative statements producing a positive effect on a person's mind, body, and spirit.

Consultation— an introduction from an Angel Specialist offering true wisdom and a fresh perspective.

Angel Specialists—a listing of angels with areas of knowledge that relate to the particular chapter topic.

Case Study—impact of experience from a powerful connection to *Angel First Aid* and The Angel Lady.

Remedies—visualization exercises and techniques designed to attain greater happiness and prosperity.

Preventive Medicine—guidelines for use of a maintenance plan with remedies and affirmations.

Prosperity Questions—queries about the benefits of connecting with the benevolent Guardian Angels.

Second Opinion—guidance from experts or professionals in fields connected to the subject of the chapter.

Miracle Story—an angelic encounter related by an individual, and the lasting impact of this experience.

Glossary of Angels is a "Who's Who" of the Angelic Realm. It can be used as a convenient directory of exceptional Angel Specialists. This list contains a short description of each angel's area of expertise. The Glossary provides a variety of understanding angels to consult for an extraordinary support system.

Keys to Prosperity is an index that functions as an integral part of the book. It is used to find specific remedies that address a desired situation or solution by referencing keywords. This guide assists in identifying the remedies or techniques that will be most beneficial for moving forward in life.

For Best Results

Take the time to develop an ongoing relationship with the angels. Invite them to participate in all facets of your life. Begin speaking with Guardian Angels in the same way you would talk to a special friend. Making them confidants is especially rewarding. Create a closer bond by sharing ideas, desires, goals, and accomplishments with them. Enlisting angelic guidance and support becomes easier through more frequent communication.

Angels like being addressed personally. Discover your angels' names to make more direct contact. An effective method to use in identifying your Archangels or Guardian Angels is to write, or ask aloud, "Angel, what is your name?" Then sit quietly and listen for an immediate audible response. Before initiating any contact with the angels, formulate your questions in advance. This helps you to maintain focus on the topic of the query.

Guardian Angels are accessible to humans at any time. They make their presence known through feelings, symbols, and dreams. A relaxed state of mind in serene, peaceful surroundings is best for receiving communication. Guardian Angels will convey messages so that the recipient hears a voice, sees a vision, or feels a presence nearby. The message will come from the angels who are providing their specific guidance. If you are working on visualizing Guardian Angels, note that they will appear in a familiar form, regardless of their shape, size, age, appearance, race, and gender.

Guidance provided by angels can easily be recognized because their messages radiate warmth and elicit calm feelings. Angels will converse in the language you speak and understand. They take on a form or persona to which you can relate. Keeping a journal of their advice and direction can prove to be beneficial. The journal will be extremely valuable for future reference.

Declarative statements, known as affirmations, will bring about desirable outcomes. Affirmations also enhance the effectiveness of any remedy. They work to focus awareness on the positive aspects of life. To create your own, start with I am _____ or I have _____ as this adds to the affirmation's potency. Repetition enhances the benefits derived from these statements.

Generating excitement for scenarios that are visualized in the remedies improves the results. Sometimes a technique will include an actual physical exercise and activity along with the visualization. Often both are required for the remedy to work. A technique may instruct you to hold the feeling for one minute. Sit quietly, allowing the experience to flow through your body. After you complete the last technique, loosen up by stretching.

Perform the remedies when it is most convenient. Follow the instructions as presented. If modification is preferable because of a circumstance such as a business trip, inconvenient setting, or time constraint, use your intuition to adapt the suggested remedies. The chapter includes nine remedies. If you cannot decide which one to do at a certain time, choose the technique that feels right or speaks to you. Be creative. Write favorite angels, affirmations, or remedies on index cards and keep them handy.

Even though angels are involved, sometimes a technique takes time to work. Be patient and persevere. When you are connecting with an angel, it is helpful to converse often. In this way you learn to differentiate between your thoughts and the advice being sent to you by the angel. For extra impact, consult the Glossary of Angels to find a Specialist that handles the area that relates to your needs. Invite Guardian Angels into your life for a prosperous lifestyle and enjoy the Angel First Aid Techniques.

Miracle Stories

Hundreds of people have shared their own angelic encounters with
The Angel Lady. The stories are recounted on television and radio
shows, or at seminars and one-on-one consultations. Although the
circumstances may differ, there is one common thread: angels are
available to provide profound support.

Angels on Duty

At a Professional Speakers Bureau Showcase, The Angel Lady met two presenters, both of whom revealed an amazing story of angelic intervention. These exceptional men are still convinced that angels were on the scene and saved their lives.

During an interesting discussion on the subject of Guardian Angels and their benevolence, JJ, a famous Chicago detective, recounted a story about angelic intervention. It happened in the line of duty. As JJ was pursuing a suspect down an alley, the fugitive paused to fire his gun at the detective's chest. JJ was unharmed—the bullet left an exit hole in the back of a new trench coat he was wearing. "Angels moved either me or the bullet!" he exclaimed.

Wayne, another speaker who would sing the national anthem at the Chicago Stadium, overheard the conversation and joined in with an incredible life-changing story. One evening after singing at the game, Wayne stopped to see friends. After he had returned to his car and was turning on the ignition to drive home, a hoodlum fired at him. The bullet hit Wayne's neck near his voice box. While waiting for paramedics and worried about his career, he thought "I hope my Guardian Angel isn't on vacation!"

Wayne recovered and eventually did sing the national anthem at the stadium once again. One year later, I heard him on the radio singing "The Star-Spangled Banner." Recalling my chat with JJ and Wayne, I found it notable how the men had credited the angels for being on duty that day and saving their lives.

Foggy Night

One memorable night when Nancy was a teenager, she discovered that she was not alone on the road. Now in her late thirties, Nancy related how a Road Angel once came to her rescue. The dramatic encounter continues to impact her career.

Seventeen years ago when I was in high school, my best girlfriends and I went to the movies. Afterward, I drove them home, dropping off Jean last. Fog rolled in as I left her home in the country. Now I had to drive thirteen miles on rural roads with decreasing visibility. Nervous, I turned on the car radio.

Eventually, it was impossible to see anything except the fog. A tall lady suddenly appeared on the road. In my headlights, I could make out her long blond hair and radiant face. She was frantically waving. After I blinked, the lady was still present, and was signaling to me with a pair of wings instead of arms.

As my car came to a screeching halt, the angel vanished—and so did the fog! Now I could see that a huge tree had fallen and was blocking the road just ahead of me. Stunned, I sat in silence for one hour, replaying in my mind every aspect of the event and its impact on me. Then I realized that the car radio had been turned off—but my fingers had never touched the dial.

Ever since that night, I know that my Guardian Angel has been traveling with me. Currently, as a buyer for a retail clothing chain, I am often required to travel. Throughout the trips, I keep a watchful eye for my angel in the middle of the road.

Out of Gas

Two best friends found themselves in a predicament on a road trip from California to Mexico. When the girls thought the chance for a solution was almost nil, a startling encounter unfolded. An unlikely hero came to their rescue in the desert.

Heading out for our road trip, we decided to drive through the first night. In one long stretch, without our having seen any signs of life for miles, we found that our car was running low on fuel. Locating a gas station in this deserted area seemed impossible. Then Sandra declared: "Angels, help us!" Within minutes, a bright light became discernible on the horizon. As we got closer, a gas station appeared. Both of us breathed a sigh of relief.

The attendant had a husky build, he wore tattered clothes, and had his long red hair pulled back in a ponytail. I immediately noted something extraordinary about him: his warm blue eyes were quite contrary to his otherwise rugged appearance. The attendant filled the gas tank without hesitation. Suddenly, we discovered that there was not enough cash for payment. He cheerfully waved us off, and we resumed our journey. As I glanced in my rearview mirror, the lights for the gas station were turned off.

On our way back to California, we took the same route so we could pay the kind attendant. We were surprised to find an empty lot, with no trace of a gas station. Still checking the area for further signs of the building, Sandra remarked, "Guess we owe the money for the fill-up to our angel attendant."

Coffee-Shop Stranger

While in college, Valerie loved the fast-paced life of New York City and its many opportunities. Looking back on that period of her life, she realizes that she owes her gratitude to a stranger. For Valerie, a chance meeting ultimately saved her life.

On a typical high-speed morning in Manhattan, I was racing to my favorite coffee shop on Chambers Street. As I walked in the door, a man tapped me on the shoulder and asked for directions. He had to find an intersection two blocks away and absolutely insisted that I accompany him to the spot. This stranger's familiar, smiling eyes reminded me of my late Uncle Joe.

This Polish man, like my Uncle Joe, spoke broken English. He could not understand my directions, although I repeated them five times. He begged me to go with him to point out the intersection in question. Having lived in the city for several years, I was normally cautious with strangers, but I felt safe with this special man. When we reached our destination, he smiled at me and disappeared into a crowd. I bolted back to the coffee shop.

On the way back, I pondered why I had trusted this individual. Without thinking, I had let my guard down with a stranger. When I got back to Chambers Street, I found chaos all around as a bomb had just exploded in the crowded coffee shop. I would have been in that café. Running back to the intersection to thank him, I searched for him frantically, to no avail. In my heart, I knew that the special man had to be one of my Guardian Angels.

Angelic Trio

Marcia, who works as a coordinator for a famous racing company, describes her angelic encounter. She kept her treasured episode to herself for a few years, as it had been so dramatic. An intervention such as this one is profoundly personal.

On a wintry night, I was working late. It had been snowing all day, with a wind chill of thirty below zero. The commute home took me through a largely undeveloped area. While on a bad stretch of road, one of my tires blew out, sending my car heading directly toward a telephone pole. Without any input from me, my vehicle turned and glided into a long driveway instead.

Quickly recovering and glancing in all directions, I realized my dilemma. The two houses in front of me were dark, and the house next door was under construction. A red car idled in its driveway. I fell multiple times as I ran toward the unfinished house. Moonlight shone through a window, revealing three figures, one male and two females, descending the stairs. All appeared stately and impressive. A pretty lady approached me and seemed to be reading my lips as I described my plight. She nodded acknowledgment, signing to both of her intensely interested companions.

All four of us got into their red car. The lady who was driving kept reading my lips as I gave instructions to my office. On arrival, she spoke out loud, "Don't forget us!" Entering the office building, I turned for a last look. There was no red car and no tracks in the snow, just me wondering, what happened?

Affirmations

I am enjoying true prosperity.

I have ample funds available.

I am overjoyed to be wealthy.

I have great happiness in life.

I am creating more resources.

1
Prosperity

CONSULTATION

Abundance in all facets of life is the definition of prosperity. Optimal health, loving relationships, and financial security are a facet of enjoying a truly prosperous existence. Sharing good fortune with other individuals brings greater personal abundance. Contentment is the genuine reward for living a truly prosperous and meaningful life.

—Katrina, Angel of Prosperity

Angel Specialists

Uriel	Archangel
Bettina	Angel of Creativity
Christine	Angel of Spontaneity
Christopher	Angel of Opportunity
Eileen	Angel of Happiness
Evelyn	Angel of Manifesting
Lawrence	Angel of Endurance
Natalie	Angel of Contentment
Rachel	Angel of Inspiration
Terina	Angel of Attraction
Timothy	Angel of Good Fortune

CASE STUDY—Road to Infinity

Looking at life through rose-colored glasses, Benny seemed willing to keep an open mind and try new concepts. This desire fed all his ambitions.

I am an on-air producer for a radio station. Interacting with guests and callers is my job. The Angel Lady is a regular guest and co-host. I decided to try Angel First Aid Techniques.

Owning a super motorcycle had been a long-time goal. With an affirmation, *I am a Mighty Money Magnet,* and a remedy, *Dollar Sign,* my task began. Putting a new twist on them, I started on a small scale by drawing some cent signs. I continued by drawing a bunch of large dollar signs. Next was adding hands and feet, working simultaneously. I used this technique at the desk in the studio. One month later, a new motorcycle was in my driveway. Another idea: use the affirmation and remedy for a big goal.

The same actions bring the same results; why not a new house? A year later, I owned a house. Another goal was a girlfriend. *I am a Mighty Love Magnet* and *Expanding Heart* became a new combination to try. Again, the same actions brought the same results! I now have a girlfriend in my life. She often calls in if The Angel Lady is on the show. Our mutual love of angels strengthens the relationship.

Benny's Steps to Success

Keep an open mind with regard to creating prosperity for yourself. Good fortune comes to people who believe and trust in the process of manifesting. Wise men try new things.

Remedies

Loving Me

The gifts and abilities individuals are given to share with the world are the same ones that indicate fulfillment of purpose. When using these gifts, life opens up. Natalie, Angel of Contentment, who has auburn hair and green eyes, is eager to hear you communicate your capabilities. Visualize sitting on a blanket in a field of wildflowers. You notice the little lavender, yellow, and white flowers in bloom. Natalie is holding a writing tablet in her hand. The angel listens as you tell her about your exceptional gifts and talents. Watch Natalie write these on a tablet in large, colorful script. This angel is proud of you for sharing your distinctive attributes with her. Take note of this pride and hold the feeling for one minute. Natalie's light-hearted smile shows her approval.

Dosage: Three times a week, after breakfast.

Angel Scrapbook

A purpose in life is selected for every human being. Each person is born with unique talents and abilities that indicate a distinct plan in life. These gifts become apparent at quite a young age. Call upon Bettina to help you create a real or imaginary scrapbook to reveal the traits you developed as a child that hinted at future special gifts. Bettina, Angel of Creativity, offers innovative ideas. Her sparkling eyes and comforting smile provide encouragement while you recall any memories that reflect the expression of your talents. Visualize or actually put snapshots of yourself as a child performing or using these abilities in this scrapbook. When you have finished, design a cover. Keep the scrapbook for insight into your life's purpose and divine path.

Dosage: Once a day, in the afternoon.

Laws for Life

The Laws of Attraction, Increase, and Restoration amplify the flow of prosperity. The Law of Attraction works as a magnet for desires, the Law of Increase stimulates manifesting powers, and the Law of Restoration can reinstate that which has been taken away. To start, have three sheets of paper ready. Terina, Angel of Attraction, is in the room. She has a dynamic personality and curly red hair. While stating each law, imagine manifesting a wish, desire, and objective. On one page, write *I invoke the Law of Attraction* fifteen times. On the next one, write *I invoke the Law of Increase* fifteen times. For a third option, write *I invoke the Law of Restoration* fifteen times. To maximize the magnetic draw of these laws, meet with Terina every day, as she has the ultimate power of attraction.

Dosage: Three times a day, after meals.

"Plenty" Exercise

When individuals believe that an ample supply of what they desire is readily available, channels to prosperity are opened. Concentrate on the word "Plenty." Think of it in the context of everything that is meaningful. Encourage Lawrence, Angel of Endurance, to stand by your side while you repeat out loud, "Plenty, Plenty, Plenty." It is most beneficial to say this word over and over again. Lawrence, with his athletic build, instructs you to contemplate "Plenty" daily. Deliberately incorporate the word in sentences throughout the day. Make up a song with it in the lyrics. Reinforce the word by writing it on a sheet of white paper fifteen times. Lawrence knows that his role is to keep your thoughts focused on the word. He brings plenty of good fortune.

Dosage: Twice a day, morning and evening.

Sack of Gold

People can generate more prosperity and abundance by collecting meaningful items. Valuable objects and other intangibles produce great benefits. Begin this visualization by envisioning, around your waist, an imaginary belt with a golden sack attached. Place several objects that are significant to you inside this sack. Rachel, Angel of Inspiration, has ideas and will assist you in selecting items for your valuable collection. Rachel's selections are innovative. Exceptional treasures appear everywhere. This angel suggests some water from a wishing well and intangibles such as happiness and contentment. Fill the golden sack until it overflows and automatically closes for the day. Wear the sack through the evening hours and transform the treasures into reality.

Dosage: Each day for two weeks, then as desired.

Pursuit of Happiness

Individuals who truly embrace life have learned how to enjoy each moment. People strive for these extraordinary times and enriching experiences. Notice Eileen, Angel of Happiness, entering the room. She looks vibrant in her lavender gown, which sets off her red hair. This angel explains: "Your point of power is in the moment! What you are thinking this instant is shaping the future." Close your eyes and take two deep breaths while contemplating the meaning of that profound statement. Commit to Eileen that you will observe future thoughts and intentions, keeping them positive and optimistic. The angel wants to join in your progress. Both of you realize that using Pursuit of Happiness will bring more joy and prosperity into your life, offering exciting moments to share.

Dosage: Twice a day, morning and evening.

Wealth on High

The acquisition of wealth happens when it is visualized frequently and reinforced with a positive belief system. Add the confidence to quickly manifest what you desire, and the world of riches opens up to you. Use this remedy with Katrina, Angel of Prosperity. Katrina is knowledgeable and confident as she begins to speak clearly. Her eyes become focused on yours while she offers this advice: "Allow WEALTH to be a significant aspect of your daily routine. Instruct your mind to recognize this word and to connect with it." Affirm WEALTH out loud with enthusiasm for five minutes twice a day. Believe that an untold sum of money has been bestowed upon you. Embrace this lifestyle while Katrina makes rewarding investments in your name.

Dosage: Twice a day, upon rising and before bed.

Love Is in the Air

Guardian Angels are present to assist people in achieving love and happiness, which are paramount for prosperity. A connection with angels brings untold joy. Form a friendship with Christine, Angel of Spontaneity. Wearing a blue gown that accentuates her sky-blue eyes, she looks serene. Together you sit on her large green blanket at the bank of a river. Christine speaks clearly: "Love is in the air." She suggests that you inhale and breathe in the love that is around you. Feel this love traveling through your whole body. Now add a brilliant color to the air, one that reminds you of the sparkling river that is flowing in front of you. Visualize this color permeating the essence of your being. Take time to enjoy the feeling. Christine has shown you how easy it is to find love and happiness.

Dosage: Throughout the day, for well-being.

Love Thy Neighbor

Money increases exponentially when it is designated for a greater purpose or the betterment of others. It is easier to generate funds when the objective is to follow through with a higher goal. Imagine Katrina, Angel of Prosperity, carrying two royal blue hula hoops in a beautiful green meadow. She hands you one, and you slip inside. This angel knows that every rotation of the hula hoop symbolically generates a huge amount of prosperous energy. This powerful force radiates through the entire community. Once it has blanketed this area with ample prosperous blessings, support the remedy with a meaningful visualization. Imagine serving a greater purpose. When finished, hand your hula hoop back to Katrina. She quickly departs, so that she can be of service to others.

Dosage: Every other day, in the morning.

Preventive Medicine

Four remedies, three times a week
Three affirmations, two times a week

Prosperity Questions

Do angels help people find their purposes in life?

People have inborn abilities that signify their destined paths in life. Several Guardian Angels are assigned to individuals to help them discover—as well as fulfill—their ordained purposes. These angels are paired with certain individuals to be a support system for their future success and path to prosperity.

Angel Specialist: Bradley, Angel of Purpose

Primary Remedy: *Angel Scrapbook*

How do angels perceive prosperity for people?

To angels, prosperity means much more than just financial wealth. Real prosperity includes richness in all areas of life: romantic love, meaningful relationships, family unity, and professional success. If all of these aspects are in sync, people enjoy happiness, fulfillment, and financial prosperity in their lives.

Angel Specialist: Katrina, Angel of Prosperity

Primary Remedy: *Wealth on High*

Second Opinion

Peter Lamas—President: Lamas Beauty Company. A beauty expert and talented makeup artist. Hosts: Beauty guidance Web site. Film credit: Titanic, *formulated waterproof makeup.*

People will be happier and will feel more fulfilled when prosperity is achieved. Then they can truly appreciate the abundant wonders of the universe. Individuals who are consciously aware of all their surroundings have a better opportunity to observe the beauty they provide. When people discover who they are and what they want to do, life is more rewarding. It becomes imperative to reflect on how to design an approach that makes a difference. Bring creativity to the profession by capitalizing on each person's inherent gifts and talents. The best advice is to study under experts in related fields, follow a path that expresses individuality, and consult with angels as they guide all of humanity through God's wisdom.

Keywords: Happiness. Beauty. Expression.

Miracle Story

Mini Message

Linda, a single mother, was experiencing a discouraging year. She had been demoted at her job, and life seemed overwhelming. Amid the chaos of the holiday shopping season, the presence of an angel offered a message of unbelievable hope.

Working and raising three young children all by myself took a great deal of time. I had to manage it alone. One dreary December day while shopping at the mall, I felt drawn to a display rack of children's clothing. Walking over to it, I saw a lady with dark curly hair peering over the rack. The woman looked very short. It seemed as if she was standing on her tiptoes just to see over the bar at the top of the rack. The lady's face radiated comfort.

Her lovely green eyes shone brightly as she shared with me, "The angels realize what is happening in your life, and they have it all under control." I looked behind the rack and saw that her feet did not touch the ground. Instead, she hovered. As I moved forward to thank her, she vanished right before my eyes.

Walking to the car, carrying the presents, I noticed a dramatic rise in the temperature. As the sun radiated its warmth, those angelic words warmed my heart. I knew that our situation would be better now. My family had a glorious holiday. We are all looking forward to a bright, sunny, and happy future together.

Affirmations

I am good at expressing ideas.

I have superior speaking skills.

I am a highly focused listener.

I have an uplifting personality.

I am a talented communicator.

2

Communication

CONSULTATION

Effective communication becomes a basic ingredient in all personal or professional interaction. When people strive to listen with real sincerity and express their thoughts clearly, they will be empowered. Mastering communication skills is imperative to prospering in life. Communication is the key for people to share authenticity.

—JENNIFER, ANGEL OF COMMUNICATION

Angel Specialists

Gabriel	**Archangel**
Christopher	Angel of Opportunity
Gunther	Angel of Fitness
Harold	Angel of Support
Irena	Angel of Patience
Jordan	Angel of Teamwork
Nicole	Angel of Negotiation
Rachel	Angel of Inspiration
Rebecca	Angel of Confidence
Sally	Angel of Perseverance
Victoria	Angel of Guidance

CASE STUDY—You've Got Mail

Knowing that the odds were stacked against her, Alyssa prayed for a solution. Her perseverance proved a to be an asset in Alyssa's career.

During my forties, I experienced a true midlife crisis. I was employed as a clerk at the local post office and yearned for a committed relationship. In my lonely heart, it felt as if life was passing me by. My dreams to make a difference in this world seemed remote. Encountering The Angel Lady with her books transformed my life: I now had the tools to find my mate and jump-start my career.

The plan was to become a postmaster and search for a soulmate. My strategy to achieve these two goals called for some affirmations. My affirmations were *I have a desire to succeed, I am a positive person,* and *I have a choice in what I do.* These became an everyday ritual.

Life soon changed for the better. I took a position as a customer service supervisor. After a transfer to a different state, I became a postmaster. To top it off, I am now dating Ernie, a man I met at the post office.

My affirmation changed to *I am happy and content.* I credit the angels with my career success and with bringing Ernie into the post office, so that the two of us could meet and discover our common interests.

Alyssa's Steps to Success

Make motivation and positive thinking a primary force in your life. Believe in yourself and all that is possible. Given the chance, angels will be present to carry you through.

Remedies

Breathing Technique

A centered individual has the advantage of being open to receiving pertinent information. Angel messages are best absorbed when in a relaxed state, usually after practicing a breathing technique. Utilize this remedy to be receptive to their guidance. Begin by welcoming Rachel, Angel of Inspiration. Dressed in a long pastel-green gown, she radiates charm. This angel instructs you to inhale through your nose and imagine the air flowing inside your head, over your brain, down your neck and spine, and directly into your tailbone. Keep a little air in your tailbone as you exhale through your mouth. Rachel happily counts as you repeat the Breathing Technique three times. She believes in your ability to receive angelic guidance. Rachel flies off to inspire others.

Dosage: Twice a day, or as desired.

Extra Vitamin C

Well-presented information will enhance effective communication. This technique uses a proven formula: complimenting, connecting, and communicating. Call on Archangel Gabriel, who is recognized as an expert in the field. Noticing his intellectual appearance, think about his proposal for genuinely effective conversing. *Compliment:* present uplifting remarks and pleasing words. Gabriel helps you to choose the words that support the complimentary effort. *Connect:* convey sincere understanding and true compassion for the person. Gabriel offers a method of expressing real empathy. *Communicate:* clearly express your point of view. The Communication Archangel adds his diplomatic touch. Now the person will be more receptive to hearing your truth.

Dosage: As desired, for healthy communication.

Little Bit of Honey

When communicating, it is advantageous to articulate thoughts or creative ideas in a manner that is clear and direct. Use a reassuring, soothing voice and a pleasant demeanor to emphasize your point. The Angel of Communication, Jennifer, has golden hair. Her easy, cheery smile reminds you to communicate in a gentle manner. One method of doing this is to genuinely compliment others. This form of communication calls for a "little bit of honey" and becomes one alternative to attracting more bees! If constructive suggestions and criticisms are necessary, Jennifer will sandwich the communication between two slices of uplifting praise. She recommends practicing the expression of compliments to friends and family. Jennifer, sweet as honey, approves.

Dosage: Once a day, or when offering advice.

Negotiating Angels

Learning the art of effective communication generates exceptional results. One secret of success is mastering written and verbal skills to promote lasting business relationships. When closing important sales or finalizing major contracts, employ this technique. To start, invite Nicole, Angel of Negotiation, to an imaginary seminar. This angel looks radiant with her brown eyes, rosy cheeks, and red lips. Picture participants wearing navy blue suits. Listening intently, the group seems interested in hearing the material mentioned in your presentation. This seminar pinpoints most pertinent issues about the use of persuasive skills. High spirits now prevail. Negotiations that ensue are favorable. Hearty handshakes signal success! Nicole departs holding several signed contracts.

Dosage: Twice a day, for sales or contracts.

Synchronized Hearts

Sometimes misunderstandings interfere with the comfort in loving relationships. When these touchy situations arise, use this remedy to iron out matters. Gunther, Angel of Fitness, appears to assist by inviting you and your partner to run with him. All three of you fall silent as your feet rhythmically pound the soft dirt on the path. At once you feel peaceful and more at ease with your partner running alongside. It seems as if you have been running for a long time, yet you still feel energized. Gunther, a rough-and-tumble angel, points out that your partner's step is in perfect sync with your own. This indicates that both of your hearts are synchronized for harmonious communication. Sit down to discuss the issues. Leave the scene with everyone smiling.

Dosage: In the evening, before dinner.

True Money Beliefs

It is paramount for individuals to recognize the difference between solid facts and false beliefs. Once the subconscious mind embraces falsehoods, the ensuing actions of the conscious mind and body are influenced. The Angel of Communication, Jennifer, arrives to help, wearing a lovely green gown. The soft-spoken angel knows that, if internalized, statements such as *Money doesn't grow on trees* along with *Easy come, easy go* leave their mark. To eliminate these ideas, Jennifer advises, "Put one hand across your forehead. Run the false statements through your mind while snapping your fingers." Then start filling your mind with statements and affirmations pertaining to prosperity. Jennifer flashes a smile to communicate her goodwill before she parts company and flies off.

Dosage: Twice a day, morning and before bed.

The Judge

Genuine prosperity can be achieved through positive thoughts and a supportive belief system. When you reach a plateau in life, think of "The Judge." He is connected to the voice in your head, feeding you criticisms and judgments. The words come from messages you heard and believed in childhood. The remarks are accompanied by a familiar feeling, indicating that you have done something wrong. Archangel Raphael recommends writing down the comments that have kept you frozen in time or unable to move forward. Shred the paper and, with it, those self-defeating thoughts. The angel suggests making a list of positive qualities that you possess. Review it twice a day for one week. Raphael offers genuine praise and approval. He is predicting your success.

Dosage: When needed, for self-confidence.

Blackboard

Individuals can amplify prosperity through clear, positive thinking. Discouraging thoughts limit affirmative action. The remedy offers a means to free yourself from counterproductive thought patterns. Harold, Angel of Support, waits by a big blackboard. Harold hands you a piece of white chalk. He says, "List any thoughts and beliefs you wish to release." Write each of them on this blackboard. Once finished, imagine a power hose cleaning off the entire board. Next, Harold hands you a piece of green chalk to write positive messages and beliefs. Sense the strength of these constructive words. Harold knows that your positive beliefs are creating positive results. He is beaming with pride at your progress. Now this angel can bring you all forms of prosperity.

Dosage: Once a day, in the morning.

Magical Doors

Successful communication opens doors to increased opportunities. Clear expression of desires assists angels in their ability to support your dreams, bringing them to fruition. For this remedy, visualize a room with six large wooden doors. Each door displays an engraved brass sign detailing one of your wishes. Making the wish come true calls for the well-qualified Christopher, Angel of Opportunity. This angel's area of expertise is demonstrating the expression of wishes in a precise manner. He says, "Be positive, specific, and absolutely clear. When you are cognizant of exactly what you desire and how to convey it, success will follow." Christopher's power propels clear requests, and every door opens! It is thrilling to enter the doors and discover many exciting angelic opportunities.

Dosage: Every other day, in the evening.

Preventive Medicine

Two remedies, two times a week
Three affirmations, three times a week

Prosperity Questions

Do angels enhance effective communication?

Angels facilitate higher levels of interaction and communication in varied forms of relationships. They provide assistance in conveying a message in a clear, precise manner. Whether thoughts are being expressed orally, in written format, or through nonverbal gestures, communication furthers understanding.

Angel Specialist: Jennifer, Angel of Communication

Primary Remedy: *Extra Vitamin C*

Can angels inspire people to cultivate ideas?

Guardian Angels encourage humans to share any inspirational and creative ideas with one another. These thoughts are valuable in any stage of personal or professional interaction. All inherent traits that people possess enhance their capability to think "outside the box," which promotes progress in their lives.

Angel Specialist: Rachel, Angel of Inspiration

Primary Remedy: *Popping Corn*

Second Opinion

Mary Jane Popp—*Host:* Poppoff *talk radio program. A child star, stage actress, and professional singer. Syndicated TV news anchor. Motivational speaker. Author:* Marilyn, Joe & Me.

Effective communication is always a two-way street. People define it as talking; rather, it is more about listening. Those who sustain a passion for people are usually great communicators. Everyone can benefit from showing genuine interest in the things that others find important. People must be open to another person's perspective. If thoughts and ideas seem important enough to be shared, then each discussion contains something of value. Those who remain focused during conversations will gather the pertinent information. Astute individuals go beyond listening, to observe body language. A smile ranks high as a communication skill. It costs nothing, takes little or no effort, and genuinely touches people.

Keywords: Communicate. Listen. Smile.

Miracle Story

Angel of Love

A precocious youngster, Jimmy, an only child, often thought about God and spiritual matters and how they would affect his future. In his bed, he would wonder if his questions would be answered when he grew up and could understand better.

My first encounter with angels happened on my eighth birthday. Sitting in my bedroom, I thought about God: what did He look like and could children ever see Him? Just then, my room brightened up and a beautiful angel slowly floated down from the ceiling. She resembled a goddess, with blond hair and a shimmering white gown. The angel had me mesmerized!

During her gentle approach, I admired her radiant face. I felt overcome with a deep love for her. She stayed in my room for one hour, never speaking, only smiling. I knew that in some way the angel was communicating this significant message to me: "I am with you forever." An imprint left on my covers where she had been sitting was evidence of her definitive presence.

Thirty years later, I had relocated for a new job to a distant city. One evening while I was working late at the office, the angel with the radiant face and unforgettable smile appeared again. The deep love I had felt as a child years ago returned. I realized the indelible imprint that this angel had left on my heart.

Affirmations

I am with a very lovable mate.

I have a prosperous soulmate.

I am having a great social life.

I have a romantic relationship.

I am in a wonderful marriage.

3

Relationships

CONSULTATION

Relationships that are based on unconditional love tend to flourish and blossom through the years. Couples who share this wholesome connection prosper. Many of these people also share a mutual purpose or mission in their lives. Good relationships continue to grow when people possess similar interests and compatible energies.

—BRIAN, ANGEL OF RELATIONSHIPS

Angel Specialists

Michael	Archangel
Bettina	Angel of Creativity
Blake	Angel of Comfort
Gordon	Angel of Focus
Lois	Angel of Clarity
Natalie	Angel of Contentment
Perrie	Angel of Music
Rebecca	Angel of Confidence
Sarah	Angel of Harmony
Tara	Angel of Love
Terina	Angel of Attraction

CASE STUDY—Thirst for Adventure

Traveling to exotic places in search of adventure was a passion for Sarah. While on vacation, a twist of fate led her to finding her soulmate.

Already a success, and earning a six-figure salary, I was the vice president of a well-known Chicago hospital. After my fortieth birthday, finding "Mr. Right" became a priority as my biological clock was ticking. While on a Club Med trip, I met Katie, who said that she had found her soulmate and secured a big promotion at her Fortune 500 company. Katie credited The Angel Lady and her remedies for romance and success. A consultation with this visionary was a real priority after my arrival back in Chicago.

Blue Sphere remedy was my first assignment from The Angel Lady. In this visualization, I had to imagine my mate inside a large blue sphere: his attitude, physical appearance, talents, health habits, and lifestyle. A written list of qualities was added. Then I attached a rocket engine to the sphere and launched it into the Angelic Realm.

Within a month, at a dinner party, I was introduced to Paul. He was a handsome, wealthy, and well-traveled man. He loved adventure; what a bonus. A month later, Paul and I were married. Since then, and with one child, we spend time globetrotting.

Sarah's Steps to Success

Miracles can occur if you are *in the right place at the right time* for love and happiness. Accept synchronicity in your life. Be available for an opportunity to find your soulmate.

Remedies

Out and About

Searching for a soulmate and significant other requires considerable thought. People wonder where to search and how to discover these special individuals. This exercise offers some direction and will be orchestrated by Brian, Angel of Relationships. When he is present, his charming personality shines. Imagine him handing you a poster board and colorful markers. Brian recommends designing a bright and colorful poster to advertise your intention to connect. Craft an invitation that will catch your soulmate's eye. Keep in mind, ideal partners will be more attracted to those who are outgoing, pleasant, and confident. Brian walks outside to post it around town. Set out each day to be the friendly, striking person who is advertised on the poster.

Dosage: Once a day, in the morning.

Likes Attract

The basic principle of the Law of Attraction is "Like attracts like"; one frequency of energy will become a magnet to a separate one of equivalent vibration. Liken it to a mirror image: what reflects out into the Universe will be returned in kind. Start this technique with the spirited Terina, Angel of Attraction, by requesting that she wait nearby as you make a list of your characteristics and best qualities. Now write a list of traits your soulmate might possess. This angel is checking your lists for compatibility. Are you ready for a soulmate, or do you require a plan for improvement? Select your strategy and move forward to gain the attributes you desire in the other person. Terina suggests repeating *I invoke the Law of Attraction.* She then flies off to locate the love of your life.

Dosage: Twice a day, when looking for a soulmate.

Entwining Hearts

When embarking on a search for a soulmate, a first impression will be essential. Balanced energy, along with an open heart, attracts an outstanding relationship. Picture Tara, Angel of Love, gracious and elegant, standing nearby. She takes your left hand, forming it into a circle by touching your middle finger to your thumb. Then taking your right hand, she moves your middle finger and thumb so they meet in the center of the first circle. These two interlocking circles symbolize two hearts entwined. As Tara observes, hold your fingers in this position for twenty seconds. Experience balance permeating throughout your mind, body, and spirit. Now you can make a good impression on those you meet. The angel is happy that you have an open heart and are ready for love.

Dosage: When needed, for a first impression.

Blue Sphere

Angels love to see people in happy relationships enjoying life with their soulmates. This becomes an invigorating experience for those fortunate enough to have connected with their perfect match. Start this technique by picturing your heart's desire sitting inside a large navy blue sphere. In this magical globe, imagine all those qualities or abilities you want your soulmate to possess. Include every detail concerning your future partner: physical traits, personality, beliefs, profession, values, and financial status. Visualize the life that you will share together; imagine every aspect. When you are finished, affix a rocket to the sphere. Jettison it to the Angelic Realm. Upon arrival, angels will search for a soulmate and intersect your paths to bring you together.

Dosage: Twice a day, after lunch and dinner.

Expanding Heart

Love makes the world go 'round and brings universal peace as well as happiness. Giving, receiving, and enjoying unconditional love is vital. Tara, Angel of Love, a tall brunette with blue eyes, shows her excitement about this remedy. Her zest for drawing is contagious, and she instructs: "Use your index finger to draw multiple hearts in the air with one continuous motion. First, begin by drawing a small heart. Second, add hearts that become larger and larger. Get into it by using your entire body for the drawing motion. Repeat the same process three times; always begin with very small hearts." Spotlight the many thoughts of love, joy, and affection running through your mind. Focus on them for one minute. Stay open to attracting more love. Tara leaves, drawing hearts.

Dosage: Twice a day, for additional love.

Sing a Song

The music in the hearts of individuals is a song of encouragement for pursuing the relationship of a lifetime. People's hearts forever carry a song of love. Be aware of this tune. Perrie, Angel of Music, who has a kind face, broad shoulders, and a rhythmic stride, enters. He acts as the maestro who orchestrates the remedy. Sit down with a pen and sheet of paper. Write a song that describes the person of your dreams. Compose lyrics that are based on what you know will provide more love and happiness. Close the lyrics with "The love I deserve is on its way." Add a simple melody, singing the love song over and over. Let the music float throughout the room. Perrie will listen to the sweet words of warmth and affection. He smiles when your song of true love fills his heart with gladness.

Dosage: Once a day, in the evening.

Motivate to Incubate

Sparking up an ongoing relationship requires a sincere intention to share fulfillment. Which ingredients of the partnership need focus? Think of each facet as a single egg nestled in a yellow basket. Lois, the enchanting, graceful Angel of Clarity, hovers above. Select one egg from the basket. Consider this an aspect of the relationship that could be improved. Imagine the egg hatching a perfect outcome for the situation. Choose one more egg and visualize the desired result. Continue until all eggs have been removed and all positive aspects realized. Lois now blesses the relationship with the proper amount of unconditional love, spontaneity, romance, and anything else that the eggs hatched for you as a couple. After igniting the spark, Lois leaves, carrying the empty yellow basket.

Dosage: Once a day, in the afternoon.

Enhancing Relationships

Couples thrive in their interactions from innovative ideas, unique experiences, and fresh perceptions. Visualizations can assist you in having a happier future. Bettina, Angel of Creativity, appears with a fragrant gardenia on the shoulder of her light blue gown. She will assist while you paint your relationship at its finest. Include special events to accentuate happiness. Utilize sounds like laughter, music, and stimulating conversations. Draw people participating in joyful activities. Add children playing, if this is a priority. The angel now has an indication of what you desire in a relationship. The painting is framed in orange, the color of manifestation. Bettina knows this work of art details the story. She quickly flies off to design a fulfilling relationship.

Dosage: Once a day, in the morning.

Forgiveness Prevails

In a mutually beneficial relationship, heartfelt forgiveness becomes an essential factor. Forgiveness does not mean condoning the other person's behavior: it means choosing the freedom to move forward in life. Requesting Archangel Michael's presence, picture the other person standing in front of you. Realize that a forgiveness exercise releases you from the drama of the situation, allowing greater inner peace. Say, "I forgive you for anything that you have knowingly or unknowingly done to hurt me." Take three deep breaths before you state, "I ask that you forgive me for anything that I have knowingly or unknowingly done to hurt you." Feel the relief. Next, consider a new perspective and fresh start. Michael appears delighted that you now have a more fulfilling relationship.

Dosage: Twice a day, on rising and before bed.

Preventive Medicine

Two remedies, three times a week
Two affirmations, four times a week

Prosperity Questions

How do Guardian Angels support love?

Life in the Angelic Realm is all about love. Through true love, the angels reinforce genuine peace and contentment. When two people experience love in its highest form, their relationship blossoms and grows bountiful. Angels nurture caring partnerships, and enhance each person's love and commitment.

Angel Specialist: Tara, Angel of Love

Primary Remedy: *Expanding Heart*

Do angels relate to the Law of Attraction?

Uniquely positioned to hear the wishes of individuals and take any appropriate actions, angels help people with the Law of Attraction. Angels realize that humans are naturally drawn to one another for loving relationships. They will often be involved in arranging these introductions which connect individuals.

Angel Specialist: Terina, Angel of Attraction

Primary Remedy: *Laws for Life*

Second Opinion

Sandy Brennan, LCSW—*Psychotherapeutic social worker of life-path and relationship issues. Founder: Earth and Spirit Creations, handcrafted jewelry with crystals and gemstones.*

Nurture a relationship as if it were a small plant, providing it with a plentiful amount of passion, attention, forgiveness, understanding, and love. Lacking these ingredients, relationships cannot grow and prosper. Relationships, like plants, will not thrive without adequate sunshine and plenty of water. Annuals and perennials are types of plants. Annuals bloom for one year while perennials will blossom year after year. Relationships can be annuals or perennials. Plants require nourishment, tender care, and pruning. Without essential water and sunshine, plants may dry out, just as a relationship may dry up. It takes an abundant supply of sustenance for every kind of plant as well as relationship to blossom.

Keywords: Attention. Love. Nourishment.

Miracle Story

Spark from an Angel

Barbara knows that an angelic feat has made it possible for her to have the husband she adores by her side every day. This encounter dramatically affected her entire family and ultimately saved the life of her truly remarkable husband, Gerald.

One part of keeping up the family farm was for Gerald to burn leaves and other items. He built a large fire pit, making it a safe distance from our house and the barn. One day Gerald burned some leaves and extinguished the fire. We had plans to go to town. Getting in the car, Gerald heard a voice say, "Check the fire pit!" He went back, and I went to meet with the accountant.

A spark had ignited the side of the barn, engulfing it in flames. Gerald quickly called our fire department. His next thought was: "Save the animals." He scrambled to free them. Overcome by heavy smoke, Gerald's heart stopped. Luckily, paramedics were already on the scene and were able to revive my husband.

Once stabilized, Gerald was transported to the local hospital. There, the doctors noticed a previously undetected heart problem requiring immediate surgery. Had angels and paramedics not teamed up earlier that day, Gerald might have suffered a fatal heart attack. We often thank the Guardian Angel who flew that fateful spark over to the barn and ultimately saved Gerald's life.

Affirmations

I am supported by my family.

I have a truly devoted family.

I am an extraordinary parent.

I have an affectionate family.

I am raising healthy children.

4
Family

CONSULTATION

The family is the first place where children are taught about the idea of prosperity. Childhood experiences influence all future decisions. It can be helpful for parents to encourage children to cherish life and to embrace a prosperous way of living. Family members who empower each other boost the level of abundance in the family.

—TARA, ANGEL OF LOVE

Angel Specialists

Raphael	Archangel
Alan	Angel of Investments
Annette	Angel of Gratitude
Barry	Angel of Strength
Brian	Angel of Relationships
Hannah	Angel of Courage
Harold	Angel of Support
Jacob	Angel of Education
Kathleen	Angel of Laughter
Melody	Angel of Self-Esteem
Patrick	Angel of Sports

CASE STUDY—Two for the Money

When his life was not what he had intended it to be, Kevin changed his outlook. He searched for an alternative and discovered it was angels.

Already in my late twenties, I hoped to be married, a father, and financially stable. Instead, I found myself single, living at home, and recently unemployed. The Angel Lady helped me find a job, doubling my previous salary. Finding a wife proved to be more work, until I met Diana, a stunning lady who took my breath away. Getting to know one another, we became aware of our dissimilar lifestyles. She craved city nightlife, and I liked the suburbs.

Consultations with The Angel Lady had improved my career, so next we worked on my plans to get married. The technique *Enhancing Relationships* helped me to visualize Diana as my wife and the mother of our two sons. To blend our opposite lifestyles, I agreed to move to the city, and she readily agreed to exit the fast lane.

In real life, Diana did accept my proposal. We invited The Angel Lady to our summer wedding. Three years later, this visionary predicted that twin boys would brighten our future. I recalled that in *Enhancing Relationships* I had seen two sons; however, I never thought that meant two boys born at the same time!

Kevin's Steps to Success

Circumstances in life often unfold differently than expected. With healthy doses of patience, compromise, and perseverance, partners in a relationship are more apt to thrive.

Remedies

Laughter Meds

The statement "Laughter is the best medicine" definitely rings true. Laughter improves body, mind, and spirit. Employ this premise to bring humor into the family. People who take life lightly and laugh often live longer, more fulfilling lives. To execute this fun remedy, visualize your family sitting around a game table. On the table you find a board game with a green pointer. Invite an angel to play the game. Kathleen, Angel of Laughter, accepts. Asked to go first, she smiles and spins the green arrow. When this arrow stops, whoever it points toward begins to laugh. Other players join in this laughter. As the game progresses, you find everyone is now laughing. When the game concludes, all family members feel the merriment in their hearts as Kathleen departs.

Dosage: Twice a day, morning and evening.

By the Sea

A more prosperous future can be achieved by releasing regrets and disappointments. Begin new endeavors with a clear mind. Envision Hannah, Angel of Courage, with her curly auburn locks blowing in the wind. She leads you down a twisting and narrow wooden dock with a sailboat at the end. The aroma of salty sea air is everywhere. Focus on some disappointments you felt while growing up. Picture a big stack of boxes close to your feet. Each one of the boxes is the perfect size to fit the memories of regrets and disappointments. Put a memory in each box, placing the boxes in the sailboat. When you are finished and only happy memories remain, the sailboat sets sail and goes out to sea. Hannah walks alongside as you both leave the dock.

Dosage: When desired, for peace of mind.

Merry-Go-Round

Personal power is a form of self-actualization that allows people to prosper. Regain personal strength to move forward in life. Imagine yourself riding on a merry-go-round with Barry, Angel of Strength. Mounted on the horses are individuals with whom you have issues to be resolved and healed. Carrying a basket, go over to the people on the carousel. Request that these people give back the intangibles taken from you. Place them in your basket. Take back your power, drive, dignity, and spirit. Watch Barry scoop these items out of the basket and place them on the crown of your head. Feel this energy traveling down your body to your navel, where it remains. You are complete once again. Get off the merry-go-round along with Barry and begin to enjoy a strong empowered life.

Dosage: Once a week, in the morning.

Gratitude Galore

Families that encourage each member's goals, visions, and dreams can prosper as a unit. Gratitude becomes a way to grow together as a family. Invite the graceful Annette, Angel of Gratitude, to join in. She is wearing a green gown and has long blond hair. To begin the remedy, gather family members around a table. Designate someone (usually a child or teenager) to make a Gratitude Box. Begin with a shoe box. Decorate it with colorful paper. Cut a hole in the top for multiple slips of paper. Individuals now write down items that have brought them happiness and for which they are grateful. All of the slips are placed in the box. Annette puts her pieces of paper in this box too. She thanks your family for letting her participate. Annette is grateful that she was invited.

Dosage: Every other day, in the evening.

Melody's Gift

A strong sense of personal value contributes to success throughout life. Confidence is a key to attaining fulfillment. The earlier this is developed, the more deeply rooted it can be. To help children build confidence, perform this technique. Melody, Angel of Self-Esteem, has fluffy golden curls, sparkling clear blue eyes, and white wings. She wears a long yellow gown. Ask the children to describe what it is that makes them feel special. They share talents, abilities, and all of their exceptional qualities with Melody. The children experience pride at possessing all their unique traits and capabilities. Now ask them to picture Melody handing them "pretend gifts" to open, play with, and keep. Children can recall these gifts to build confidence. Melody flies off to go shopping for exciting toys.

Dosage: Three times per week, or as desired.

Double Their Money

Financial independence can be achieved through knowledge of and proficiency in economics. Wise parents will educate their children to have an appreciation of finances. To start this remedy, welcome Alan, Angel of Investments, who is fiscally savvy. He will act both stern and gentle, knowing that each has its place. Alan proposes to help children learn to save money. When youngsters obtain money from gifts or as an allowance, permit them to give you a portion to save for the future. Allow them to get acquainted with Alan, as this angel will be beside them while making future financial decisions. When children learn to handle their own funds, excitement builds. Alan approves, realizing that as these children become adults, they are well versed in economics.

Dosage: As required, for teaching children.

Angel Tutors

Schoolwork and extra curricular activities may be overwhelming to students regardless of their overall aptitude. Astute parents provide their children increased opportunities for intellectual development. Suggest that your children make requests of their Guardian Angels. It would be helpful if they called on Jacob, Angel of Education, and Patrick, Angel of Sports, for assistance. Both of these caring angels are smart and industrious. They eagerly tackle assignments. Young scholars can ask Jacob to sit beside them while studying and taking tests. Sports enthusiasts imagine Patrick as a member of their team. Patrick cheers youngsters on to victory. Angel Tutors are prepared to mentor students at a moment's notice. They coach athletes to excel, reaching for the gold.

Dosage: Daily, during the school year.

Hand Hold

Family members who stay centered are better equipped to sustain balance in their lives. Establishing equilibrium is vital to everyone. Harold, Angel of Support, with his dark hair and green eyes, enters the room. This angel delights in your family's well-being. He has a centering technique to share. To start, fold one hand over the other hand's fingertips, palm to palm, exerting mild pressure. Push down gently toward the wrist at least five times. Repeat this procedure on the thumb. Duplicate the process on the opposite hand. Place one hand, palm down, on the crown of the head, and press another five times. This remedy works for all family members and is wonderful as a method to calm children. Harold, ready to depart the premises, searches for another family to balance.

Dosage: Once a day in the morning, or as desired.

Statement for Love

Angels and people can team up to promote balance and harmony in family relationships. Guardian Angels eagerly help with all areas if you put your faith in them. Angels encourage this remedy, which is based on a premise that affirmations, properly phrased, produce rewarding results. Brian, Angel of Relationships, is a distinguished-looking angel. He asks you to choose the circumstances you desire to improve and the family member who could benefit from greater understanding. In an affectionate voice, say: *The relationship that I have with my (mother, father, sibling, child, grandchild) generates happiness, harmony, and peace of mind. We are truly blessed with unconditional love.* Repeat these statements with affection. Brian is pleased with the newfound family unity and profound harmony.

Dosage: Twice a day, or when needed.

Preventive Medicine

Three remedies, two times a week
Two affirmations, five times a week

Prosperity Questions

Should families invite angels into their lives?

The Angelic Realm is a dimension where angels play an important role in interacting with each other as a loving family. On Earth, all children learn to love and make spiritual connections. Every family member thrives from maintaining a relationship with angels. This will augment the family's prosperity.

Angel Specialist: Sarah, Angel of Harmony

Primary Remedy: *Gratitude Galore*

How do angels help families maintain love?

A continual flow of devotion and affection is essential for families to blossom and flourish. Angels encourage each family member to be aware of the other person's feelings. This contributes to warmer exchanges of communication within a family unit. Angels provide unconditional love and their blessings.

Angel Specialist: Brian, Angel of Relationships

Primary Remedy: *Statement of Love*

Second Opinion

Cheryl Maraffio—*Elementary school resource specialist: Directs a school-safety and crime-prevention workshop. Former compliance expert in the field of securities and commodities.*

Families influence the security and integrity of each child. Many of the social ills in our society could be rectified if parents agreed to a role of leadership, allowing children to learn by example. Families are more cohesive or unified if members will accept responsibility. Dependability can be attained with these four steps: (1) always tell the truth; (2) follow the rules; (3) help out when asked; (4) do what has to be done before being asked. Good decisions require time for weighing pros and cons and considering all possible consequences. Listen to that "little voice" that knows right from wrong. Pay close attention. Families that follow these basic principles offer members a head start toward attaining happiness.

Keywords: Leadership. Responsibility. Decisions.

Miracle Story

Miracle in the Making

Josie and Peter had been trying to have a child for five years. How they were eventually able to become parents is an angelic miracle. Their nine-year-old son is a delightful child and has been told why his parents had a special name for him.

Doctors warned me that my medical condition required surgery, and that I would be unable to have children. In the hospital the night before surgery, I awoke and saw a Victorian staircase. Descending this staircase was a lady wearing a nurse's uniform. She assured me that I would be "just fine" and affirmed that a baby boy would soon make an appearance in my family.

At home that night, Peter answered the doorbell to find a man claiming that he had car trouble. After this man completed his call for a taxi cab, he said, in a deep voice, "Your wife is just fine." Heading toward the door, the stranger looked right at Peter and said, "My name is Joshua." My husband, totally perplexed, wondered how the man knew about my health issues.

After surgery the next day, Peter and some doctors were at my bedside. It seemed that the medical situation visible on X-rays the day before was no longer apparent. I was "just fine." Two years later, I gave birth to a baby boy, as predicted. We named our baby Joshua after the angel who visited my husband.

Affirmations

I have a sweet and loving pet.

I am gifted in healing my pet.

I have healthy and hardy pets.

I am enjoying my lovable pet.

I have happy and cuddly pets.

5

Pets

CONSULTATION

The true affection that owners have for their special pets is transcendent and uplifting. The love that pets have for their owners is unconditional. Loyal and compassionate, animals love with their entire being. Pets as companions contribute nuturing, comfort, and support. People prosper from this really easy, unlimited flow of love.

—THOMAS, ANGEL OF ANIMAL CARE

Angel Specialists

Raphael	Archangel
Blake	Angel of Comfort
Christine	Angel of Spontaneity
Eileen	Angel of Happiness
Florence	Angel of Compassion
Irena	Angel of Patience
Laramie	Angel of Discovery
Maureen	Angel of Time
Mirra	Angel of Healing Arts
Paula	Angel of Energy
Peter	Angel of Health

CASE STUDY—Finding Malcolm

Living in the country with her family gives Cindy a chance to have cats, dogs, and horses. She takes care of as many as ten animals.

I am a person who feels especially content and secure with animals around me. My friends intuitively realize this and drop strays off at the house. Malcolm was one of those cats. A gray-and-white tabby, he would never leave my side. Like my shadow, Malcolm followed me, inside the house and down the driveway.

Malcolm's routine was to be out at night and return in the morning. One day, though, he was not waiting for me. We searched everywhere we knew without finding a trace of my companion. Then I checked an Angel First Aid book and found Laramie, Angel of Discovery. He can locate lost pets. I began to pray, pleading with Laramie to find my cat. I called The Angel Lady to alert her. Three days later, there was still no visible sign of Malcolm.

The following night, it rained all night. I prayed much harder. In the morning, I opened our door to find Malcolm waiting. He was dry! Neither mud nor water could be seen or felt on him anywhere. The Angel Lady confirmed that Laramie had intervened. He had dropped Malcolm off; safe, sound, and dry.

Cindy's Steps to Success

Invite angels to lend a helping hand whenever circumstances seem impossible. Always put your trust in them, for their support is truly a blessing. Believe in the power of angels.

Remedies

I Am Home

Preparing a pet to adapt to its new home and family is important in ensuring a beneficial transition. Help the animal feel welcome and secure in its unfamiliar new surroundings. Being a compassionate, considerate, and caring angel, Thomas is delighted with your idea to establish a warm, comfortable environment for the new addition to the family. Thomas, Angel of Animal Care, explains that animals will form an association by adapting to new places through all their senses. Lead the pet through the house and introduce it to the new surroundings. Calmly talk to your pet and show it those places and things that are important to you. Allow your new pet to investigate a few of these areas. Recognizing what you find meaningful helps it to internalize "I am home."

Dosage: As desired, with new pets.

Chow Time

A regular schedule is advisable for humans and animals alike when food and digestion are involved. The pattern of a set time to eat can make life easier for owners and pets. This technique helps keep the pet at a healthy weight and teaches the pet not to beg while humans are eating or sitting at a dinner table. Begin by selecting a time that is convenient for you to feed the pet each day. This time should not vary too much; no more than one hour in each direction is the best. Maureen, Angel of Time, keeps you on a schedule. With her raven hair and brown eyes, she radiates charm. Work together as a team. Get your pet excited about eating. Call it "Chow Time" and say the words clearly before feeding and your pet will know what to expect. Maureen is happy to appear twice daily.

Dosage: Each day, while training a new pet.

Pet Bonding

The bond between humans and animals is incomparably rewarding and fulfilling. Guardian Angels consider pets a wonderful blessing. One way to enjoy a stronger connection with your pet is to practice mind-to-mind communication. Archangel Gabriel is eager to work with you. As the Archangel of Communication, Gabriel's outgoing personality gives you confidence to perform the remedy. To begin, concentrate while staring into your pet's eyes. Project a beam from your forehead to the animal's forehead, sending it a message with a gentle command. Take notice of any slight change in the pet. Does the animal send back a message of any kind? Is there a visible sign of understanding, such as a purr or lick? Gabriel loves telepathy for bonding purposes. Your pets will too!

Dosage: Twice a week, for bonding.

Triple Digits

Anything owners can do to benefit the lives of the pets they love is a blessing. The care that owners provide their pets can be improved by practicing this remedy. Start by placing the three middle fingers of your right hand on the back of your pet's neck. Rub vigorously, yet gently. Your fingertips move in all directions. Since the remedy will generate warmth and contentment in your pet, Florence, Angel of Compassion, is present to facilitate. Triple Digits brings you and your pet additional bonding. Florence, an unusually compassionate angel, has brown hair that hangs down her back. Her smile warms your heart in the same way that doing Triple Digits warms up your pet. Compassion, Florence's specialty, keeps her busy visiting pets throughout the world.

Dosage: Three times a week.

Angelic Pets

Animals possess an exceptional instinct that is far superior to any similar sense present in humans. Applying these heightened senses, sharp and keen, a pet can be the guide to a presence in your room. If the pet stares or barks without a visible image present, then stand back and let your mind go beyond what is logical: there is definitely an angel presence in the room. Concentrate on the angel to receive a message from the Angelic Realm. Visualize this angel and notice how it appears to you. If your pet moves its head, follow its line of sight. Since angels float, they will rarely remain in one area for any length of time. Follow the pet's gaze when it is looking around, and welcome these angels into the room. Encourage these guardians to stay, and listen for their insightful messages.

Dosage: Whenever pets sense angels.

Pet Healing

Sometimes animals require extra healing to maximize their energy. Healthy pets are happy pets, and owners love to find them jumping around and running playfully. When this is not happening, check in with Thomas, Angel of Animal Care. He will discover the way to boost healing. The angel is large in stature and brings along special healing power for your pet. Thomas and you can practice this easy technique together. Visualize the animal in perfect health. You are both playing outdoors with your pet, having a great time. Thomas is delighted to join in and perform the healing. He sprinkles royal blue powder on the animal, concentrating on specific areas. Focus on the image for one minute to reinforce his healing power. Trust angelic therapy to heal your pet.

Dosage: Once a day, or as needed for healing.

Touch of Love

Families with pets know the animals benefit from healing sessions and from gentle loving. Call upon Mirra, Angel of Healing Arts, to care for your pets. Begin the remedy by placing both hands around the belly or middle of the animal, and send love toward it. Envision Mirra pouring a sparkling blue light into the crown of your head. It moves through your neck, shoulders, arms, and hands, transferring into the pet's body. Next, picture your animal filled with this same sparkling blue light. The blue color has a powerful healing energy. Allow at least five minutes for each session. If working on a larger animal, place both hands directly on the spot requiring healing. For birds and fish, place hands on the cage or tank. Mirra smiles when pets have good health and plenty of unconditional love.

Dosage: Daily, for extra love.

Sleep Meds

People who are lucky enough to have a cat or dog as a companion have a built-in solution for a sleepless night: simply watch your pet while it sleeps. Eileen, Angel of Happiness, with her kind blue eyes twinkling, is preparing to let you know her secret. In her words, "If it is difficult for you to sleep, watch a pet sleeping. It will calm you down immensely. Focus on a pet's rhythmic breathing cycle until a sense of peace permeates your entire being. Since a pet becomes so invested in sleeping, extraneous thoughts do not interfere. Because cats and dogs live in the present, they focus on what is happening right now." Eileen recommends watching your pet slumber during the day, too, for more peace. Ponder this angel's wisdom and her guidance. Sleep on it!

Dosage: Daily, for rest and peace.

Lost Pet

Pets are treasured members of the family, showing affection to all those who care for them. When pets wander off and do not return, their owners will attempt whatever becomes necessary to locate the animal. Laramie, Angel of Discovery, is a no-nonsense type of guy and gets the job done. Contact Laramie to find (*name of pet*). See your pet in its bed or favorite spot. Finally, repeat this affirmation, *Our (name of pet) comes back on its own or is found and returned to us quickly.* An angelic partnership has been formed. You and the angel are now working together as a team to locate the pet. Laramie provides guidance and fresh ideas on where to search. After the pet has been found and returned home, thank Laramie for making the family whole and complete once again.

Dosage: As necessary, to find a pet.

Preventive Medicine

Four remedies, three times a week
Two affirmations, three times a week

Prosperity Questions

How do angels perceive people having pets?

Owners and pets who love each other exemplify a supreme level of loyalty and affection. When owners nurture their pets and provide limitless and unconditional care, the animals will respond in kind. The angels know about the bond that humans share with their pets and bless these fundamental connections.

Angel Specialist: Joseph, Angel of Joy

Primary Remedy: *Pet Bonding*

Do pets and animals have Guardian Angels?

Every pet and animal is under the care and protection of Thomas, who is the Angel of Animal Care. Unlike humans, there is just one Guardian Angel for all pets. Owners rely on Thomas to assist them with health and training. Although Thomas plays a significant role, all angels watch over pets and other animals.

Angel Specialist: Thomas, Angel of Animal Care

Primary Remedy: *Angelic Pets*

Second Opinion

Berrie Salbego, DVM—*Medical director: Manager for a veterinary clinic for a national corporation; exotic-animal surgeon. President of Phi Alpha Beta Veterinary Honorary Society.*

As ever-faithful companions, pets express their unconditional love, loyalty, and eagerness to please. They want to be included in family activities and enjoy interacting with their owners. In turn, pets can help to improve the health of the people around them by reducing stress and lowering blood pressure. Often people believe that their pets have souls and are spiritual beings. Owners sometimes notice that their animals possess a form of telepathy. Animals are intuitive and rely on most of their senses to comprehend and respond. They remain in the present, reminding their owners about the benefits of mindfulness. Pets provide comfort in helpful, gentle, and nurturing ways. They are a blessing beyond words.

Keywords: Faithful. Loyal. Intuitive.

Miracle Story

Angel in Disguise

The Angel Lady's cat was a gift, and she named him Fangorn after a forest in The Lord of the Rings. A short-haired kitten, he grew to be an extraordinary blessing for many clients. Fangorn became an effective partner of the healing team.

Fangorn greeted clients when they arrived for a session. To be first to check them out was a responsibility he did not take lightly. He instinctively knew if a client needed his help. Providing comfort became his special niche. A head-butt and loud purr were his trademarks. For those who were happy, he left the room.

During a session, Sharon displayed pictures of four cute children. As she placed each of them on the couch, little Fangorn sat himself close to Sharon. While Sharon spoke about Tommy, her child who had died, Fangorn gently stretched out his left paw and touched the face in the child's photograph. Sharon also had lost a baby girl. While talking about baby Amanda, Fangorn pointed at her picture. She soon started to talk about her two living children's sports activities and appeared peaceful. Fangorn predictably left the room.

Being more like an angel than a cat, Fangorn knew what to do and just when to do it. This special cat could raise spirits or elicit a smile by showing affection at the right moment. Fangorn was a pet that was behaving like an angel in disguise.

Affirmations

I am finding new friendships.

I have compassionate friends.

I am enjoying my new friends.

I have happy, devoted friends.

I am attracting reliable friends.

6
Friendship

CONSULTATION

Lasting friendships shape lives by setting a solid foundation for the creation of happy, meaningful relationships. People who pursue establishing these heartful associations during their lives will have companionship and camaraderie. Good friendships are personal connections that can pave the way for mature, purposeful partnerships.

—KEVIN, ANGEL OF FRIENDSHIP

Angel Specialists

Gabriel	**Archangel**
David	Angel of Camaraderie
Eileen	Angel of Happiness
Gordon	Angel of Focus
Irena	Angel of Patience
Lawrence	Angel of Endurance
Rachel	Angel of Inspiration
Theodore	Angel of Kindness
Theresa	Angel of Empowerment
Timothy	Angel of Good Fortune
Valerie	Angel of Understanding

CASE STUDY—Lemonade Stand

Moving out of the situation where he found himself and into one he craved became Daniel's challenge. He turned lemons into lemonade.

Every part of my life seemed average. An old car, a dull job, and a tiny apartment kept my life mediocre. "Boring" fit me perfectly. I wanted more from life. Moving up in the world and meeting my ideal woman was a priority. Although fate had left my life in neutral, it was definitely time to shift into high gear.

While I was driving my secondhand Chevy, on a routine day, an intriguing interview on a radio show held my attention. The guest, The Angel Lady, was providing guidance on how angels help people achieve financial independence and find true love. My first phone consultation made a big difference in my life.

Angel First Aid provided me with the tools that I needed to brighten my future. I faithfully practice an assortment of remedies: *Winning Friendships, Career Bliss,* and *Backbone.*

Today, a new car is what I drive to my rewarding new job. Tina is my new girlfriend and my new home provides me with greater comfort. My life is definitely in high gear!

Daniel's Steps to Success

Changing the direction of your path from average to extraordinary is easy, with angelic encouragement. Staying focused on improving your life creates exceptional happiness.

Remedies
Winning Friendships

Solid friendships develop between individuals who are invested in one another's achievements. Being supportive and encouraging can pay off in the future. When invested in the happiness of friends, the bonds you share increase. Use the remedy to boost the relationship. Observe Theodore, Angel of Kindness. He has wonderfully bright blue eyes. The angel encourages you to do something generous or "unexpected" for your friends. Start the caring remedy by thinking, "How can I make their day as well as how can I make them smile?" Consider what act of random kindness would make a difference in your friends' lives. Brightening their day can be wonderful as well as immeasurable. Make it happen! These friendships will be enriched by your deeds.

Dosage: Three times a week, in the afternoon.

Catch an Opportunity

People flourish from being recognized and acknowledged for their talents and outstanding accomplishments. Friendships offer ideal opportunities to give people compliments. To begin this technique, welcome Eileen, Angel of Happiness. Now visualize all your friends wearing signs that say "Make me feel special!" Grab each chance to make that happen. The Angel Eileen suggests: "Share with friends your feelings on what they say or do that is extraordinary. Let them know how much you appreciate the way they treat you." Be lavish with your compliments. Praise your friends for their abilities. This positive energy radiates outward to them and ultimately returns to you. Everyone involved benefits. Eileen, looking very pleased, exclaims "Go for it!"

Dosage: Whenever possible, to win friends.

On the Fast Track

Attracting good friends or a compatible social group often requires action and focus. If circumstances call for new friends because of a move to a new house, a change of schools, or a job-related transfer, take time to perform this useful remedy. Visualize yourself running around a large track with other runners who represent your future friends. Lawrence, Angel of Endurance, who is tall and fit, appears and runs with you. The angel says, "You can catch up." Lawrence provides his support and encouragement as you begin to run faster. Getting a burst of energy, you speed up and join the pack. Evaluate the runners and choose the ones with complementary interests and compatible energies. Lawrence praises your efforts in finding new friends and runs off into the distance.

Dosage: Once a day, in the afternoon.

Brain Fog

Lasting friendships develop when people are able to be themselves. Occasionally, just prior to meeting with friends, you are focused on other things that are taking place in your life. Since friends deserve your full attention, this remarkable remedy prepares you to be alert and available to your friends. Gordon, Angel of Focus, is hovering nearby, ready to assist. While sitting or standing, extend your arms forward, palms facing down. Spread your fingers and wiggle them rapidly and energetically for seven seconds. You may experience a flow of energy rising through your body. Gordon realizes that your thoughts and attention have become focused and your mind is now crystal-clear. He has served his purpose. Gordon flies off on golden wings to return to the Angelic Realm.

Dosage: Throughout the day, to refocus.

Clearing the Slate

People sustain good relationships by forgiving the transgressions of friends. Learn to forgive, release, or get over past situations by use of this remedy. Theodore, Angel of Kindness, with his brown hair and olive skin, is here to offer support. He hands you a thick pad of paper. Write down one dilemma or situation you desire to remove from a friendship. This is the time to totally eliminate unhappy and uncomfortable feelings. When finished, cross out the words. Shred the sheet of paper. Quickly throw it away. Angel Theodore watches and praises your deliberate actions. He commends you for working on the friendship. Begin to think kindly about your friend. Picture the two of you in good spirits, sharing a hug. Theodore wants a hug too. A group hug follows.

Dosage: Twice a week, in the evening.

Screen Saver

Enjoying friends often means having some discretionary funds that allow you to attend sports and social events. This game will help in that endeavor. The remedy works to increase the cash available for various activities. Timothy, Angel of Good Fortune, handsome and smart, sits near you playing a computer game he designed. Imagine the screen bursting with bright and vivid graphics, exhibiting times you were without funds or the means to enjoy friends. When these images jump out, quickly snap your fingers and hit DELETE. With a blank screen in view, Timothy changes it to exciting images which depict friends having fun together. The friends can be traveling and attending an event that requires expensive tickets. Hit SAVE to keep these images. Game over. YOU WIN!

Dosage: Twice a week, in the evening.

Time Out

The friendships in our lives have a strong impact on our outlook or happiness. The people we call friends fill multiple purposes. These individuals take on different roles that can change from day to day. Friends enjoy spending time together and sharing personal insights with one another. Friends occasionally have differences of opinions that make being together seem uncomfortable. Taking a *Time Out* might be beneficial. Sit quietly and wait for directions. Two tender angels enter the room. Irena, Angel of Patience, helps you to open your heart to listen deeply to your friends. The other angel, Valerie, has compassion, as she is the Angel of Understanding. She teaches you how to gain a better perspective and revive the friendship once again. These angels know balance has been restored.

Dosage: In the morning, on awakening.

Backbone

People experience rewarding friendships when they exhibit respect for themselves as well as others. Use this empowering technique to develop stronger boundaries and set limits for new and established friendships. Imagine Theresa, Angel of Empowerment, standing by your side; her sweet smile comforts you. Picture the energy in your body moving from the front, chest and abdomen, toward the back and into the spine. This energy remains in your backbone. Respect will be yours to give and receive. Theresa states: "If you encounter a situation where resolve or personal power is required, call on me to stand beside you." Theresa is amazed by your dynamic persona and newfound strength. She offers her continual support, desiring to become a lifelong ally.

Dosage: Once a day, in the morning.

Popping Corn

Friendships offer opportunities to explore untapped creative ideas. Generate a wealth of ideas with your friends. Seek assistance from Rachel, Angel of Inspiration. Share the technique collectively with friends, or use it exclusively as a way to develop ideas. While you are making popcorn, all kernels begin to pop as they reach the right temperature. Start with a clean corn-popper by clearing your mind. Be free and spontaneous as you brainstorm. Raise the temperature of these extraordinary fun thoughts and concepts. This angel wants each kernel popped completely. Now write down innovative ideas that pop into your head. Rachel offers her novel revelations. When you are finished brainstorming and each friend has participated, it is the best time to add a good amount of butter and salt.

Dosage: Twice a week, or when with friends.

Preventive Medicine

Two remedies, three times a week
Four affirmations, two times a week

Prosperity Questions

Can angels help people find friends?

Good friendships expand people's lives by providing closeness and companionship. Guardian Angels enjoy making solid connections between individuals who share compatible thoughts and interests. Assisting friends in the formation of long-lasting relationships is a genuine delight for Guardian Angels.

Angel Specialist: Kevin, Angel of Friendship

Primary Remedy: *On the Fast Track*

How do angels help friendships last?

Angels regard bonds of friendship as essential to the well-being of individuals. Long-lasting friendships can provide security and trust among groups of people. Angels assist friends in staying connected and in touch for meaningful interactions. They love watching good friends strengthen deeper connections.

Angel Specialist: Theodore, Angel of Kindness

Primary Remedy: *Winning Friendships*

Second Opinion

Pat Baccili, PhD—*Radio show host/producer: "Aspiring Woman of the Year." (Aspire magazine) Recipient: Evvie award; International Crystal award. Orchestrates: Life Coaching seminars.*

Early friendships play an intricate role in shaping relationships that people share as adults. These friendships strengthen people's lives. Human beings naturally possess an incredible power to attract new and lasting friendships. There is a keen desire within us to connect with people in a profound manner. The three major components of all friendships are commitment, understanding, and loyalty. When friends interact at this heartfelt level, an exceptional bond develops between them. This bond creates an eventual uniting of these souls that transcends outside interference. Lifelong friends will enjoy an honest appreciation for one another. These strong connections are supreme and beyond verbal expression.

Keywords: Friendship. Commitment. Compassion.

Miracle Story

The Pink Lady

Legally blind, Emily traveled alone for the first time by airplane. A trip from Minneapolis to Cleveland had been planned so she could visit her daughter for the holidays. Emily found that a twist of fate meant an unexpected adventure for her.

Purchasing a round-trip, nonstop airline ticket direct to the Cleveland airport was important for my security. In my late seventies and a widow, I was traveling alone. A vision impairment made this flight seem daunting. The flight to Cleveland went smoothly; the trip back did not go well. We landed in Chicago. Befuddled, I got off the plane. Upset and slowed down by poor eyesight, I went to find a ticket counter. Finding one, I pleaded for a seat on the next plane to Minneapolis. Agents said that I would have to wait until morning.

I was astounded when I saw—perfectly—the figure of a lady standing far away. This lady caught my eye, as she was dressed in a shocking pink suit with a matching hat. She held my attention, since hot pink is not a color I connect with Christmastime.

Suddenly, the lady appeared by my side, escorting me to another ticket counter. Somehow she related each detail of my dilemma, securing a seat for me on the next plane to Minneapolis. The "Angel in Pink" smiled at me before she turned and then vanished. I never had a chance to express my gratitude for her kindness.

Affirmations

I am full of vitality and vigor.

I have a strong, healthy body.

I am energized and powerful.

I have pep and robust energy.

I am incredibly physically fit.

7
Health

CONSULTATION

With a vibrant aura and powerful energy field, individuals can lead their lives with optimum health and true vitality. Such energy instills a liveliness that makes individuals more attractive. With extra vibrancy, people experience a strong desire to pursue personal and professional endeavors. This leads to a more prosperous lifestyle.

—PAULA, ANGEL OF ENERGY

Angel Specialists

Raphael	**Archangel**
Barry	Angel of Strength
Esther	Angel of Vitality
Florence	Angel of Compassion
Gunther	Angel of Fitness
Madeline	Angel of Teachers
Patrick	Angel of Sports
Peter	Angel of Health
Robert	Angel of Balance
Sherrill	Angel of Stability
Tyler	Angel of Abundance

CASE STUDY—Identity Crisis

In her mid-forties and young at heart, Carol had been yearning for an extra dimension to her life. Angels played a major role in her success.

Carving out a path in life was daunting. I grew up on a farm with nine siblings, and being a mother of two teenagers did not turn out to be any easier. Finding The Angel Lady made life much better. Our first phone session made a difference. I started on a path toward discovering my purpose. Then I began to believe in myself. The Angel Lady suggested that I trust my intuition.

Merry-Go-Round was my first remedy to heal troubled past relationships, and *Likes Attract* followed for romance. The affirmations I used, *I am loved and appreciated,* along with *I am creating the life of my dreams,* were on my daily agenda. To choose a career, I practiced *Break Room.* In this visualization, I saw myself talking with people at a business convention and making them happy.

Two years later, what I envisioned became reality. As a motivational speaker, I traveled to Chicago and visited with The Angel Lady. After the flight home, a voice insisted that I walk the dog at the lake by my house. This is where I met Jerry, a man walking his three dogs on the same path. My soulmate and I found each other.

Carol's Steps to Success

Find your career path by visualizing yourself pursuing a purposeful life doing the work that you desire. For guidance, always trust your own intuition and advice from angels.

Remedies
Vitality Plus

Personal strength dramatically improves with optimal energy flow. This stamina originates from a balanced metabolic convergence of energy. Esther, Angel of Vitality, approaches. She is a petite angel with blue eyes and curly red hair. Esther instructs: "Place your left hand over your throat and drop the right hand to your side with all fingers pointing down toward the floor. Start by rotating your right wrist in a clockwise direction, forming a circle. Thirty rotations is a perfect number to complete the remedy." Esther counts along with you. After completing these thirty rotations, observe the difference in your energy level. All results are cumulative, and it is valuable to perform Vitality Plus daily. Let the angel help to motivate you and act as your angelic personal trainer.

Dosage: Every day, after your largest meal.

Angel Wings

Diaphragmatic breathing with conscious intention expands energy flow and supplies more oxygen to the brain. This form of breathing also releases endorphins. Peter, Angel of Health, who has dark hair and a calming demeanor, is hovering above. Now start this remedy by standing comfortably. Inhale through your nose to the count of five, while reaching your arms up toward this angel. Exhale slowly through your mouth as you count to five again, bringing your arms down to your sides. After a third repetition, feel the vibrant energy flowing through your entire body. Peter is hovering lower now and offers congratulations. The angel is very pleased and proud of you, exclaiming, "You have earned your angel wings!" Peter is cheering enthusiastically.

Dosage: Before breakfast, or as desired.

Energy Tap

Exhibiting enthusiasm for life improves the likelihood of attracting good fortune. Develop real stamina and approach life with vitality. Paula, the vivacious Angel of Energy, appears, wearing a gown of crimson silk. She directs you to place a hand over your navel, and with the other hand, tap each of these acupressure points ten times: below your collarbones right where they connect to the breastbone, above your upper lip, and beneath the lower lip. Change hands and repeat. Recharging mental and physical batteries starts your energy flowing and keeps it balanced throughout the day. Notice the extra buoyancy. You feel vital and full of pep, enchancing your ability to generate good fortune. Paula is delighted that you appear enthusiastic.

Dosage: Once a day, morning or evening.

Cardio Dance

Prosperity can be readily improved through movement and dance each day. This type of action keeps the mind and body in excellent health. Begin by signaling for Patrick, Angel of Sports, to join you in this remedy. On cue, Patrick, a handsome angel with an athletic build, broad shoulders, and bountiful energy, laces up a new pair of dancing shoes. Play some music and start to freestyle dance. Smile, as if the two of you were performing onstage for an audience. Stay involved with the movement and sway to the beat. Tune in to your body as it instinctively generates its own rhythm and flow. Express your thoughts and feelings through dance. Patrick, who becomes a full-time cardio dance partner, continues doing an upbeat freestyle. When Patrick leaves, he exits stage left.

Dosage: Three times a week, in the morning.

Twisting

Everyone prospers from movements that create a zest for life. This action generates energy that flows in a positive way and enhances the body, mind, and spirit. Welcome Madeline, Angel of Teachers, whose spunky personality makes it easy to perform this technique for healing and fun. First, she suggests practicing the exercise while lively music is playing. Second, Madeline advises you to smile and think joyful thoughts. To start, stretch your arms out to your sides, keeping them at shoulder level. Twist at the waist while swinging both of your arms rhythmically from side to side. Madeline wants to be a Twisting partner. This angel adds a "Twist" of her own by imitating this motion with her wings. Twisting is so much fun that Madeline laughs.

Dosage: Throughout the day for a boost.

Shake It Up

Developing a balanced energy flow prepares people for life's many opportunities. Become primed for more happiness in every way by calling upon Sherrill, Angel of Stability. She seems to have a glow about her and is eager to join in on the fun. Sherrill wants you to be dynamic and energized by this remedy. Take your shoes off and sit on a comfortable couch. Wiggle your toes for ten seconds. Loosen your ankles by rotating each foot in a circular motion. Wiggle your body for ten seconds. Just let loose. Shake it up. The path has been cleared for the energy to flow freely throughout your body. Sherrill advises using this remedy daily. She will return for encouragement when new opportunities arise. Watch for her to appear in the near future, as she will be a part of your life forever.

Dosage: Each day, in the middle of the day.

Medium Blue

Bright colors boost energy flow; they can also reinstate full balance. Used as a tool for good health, colors produce maximum power for healing or mending. This technique acquaints you with a resource that angels use on a regular basis. Medium blue, their favorite color for healing, is the key to vital energy and curative first aid. Envision Peter, Angel of Health, appearing to "take you under his wing." He has a comforting manner that makes you feel more peaceful. Peter infuses your body with medium blue. This color reaches your heart first, expanding in all directions throughout your body. When each cell is saturated, keep the color in your body for one minute before letting it flow out through your feet. Peter bestows his exceptional type of Angel First Aid and then quickly departs.

Dosage: Three times a week, or as needed.

Power of Eight

There are occasions when a specific area of the body requires extra attention and healing. Let angels know if a particular region needs some additional work. Archangel Raphael appears. His gentle and calm approach washes over you like a soothing wave of peace. The Archangel says, "Take three deep breaths and let your body relax. Now put the index finger of your right hand on the area requiring healing and make figure-eights for ten rotations." The other angels arrive to watch you practice this technique. They begin projecting a lavender light onto the affected region. This combination of figure eights and lavender light has an incredible healing power. Raphael and the other angels leave you feeling more comfortable, healthier, and equipped to meet the world.

Dosage: Throughout the day, for healing.

Power Surge

When personal drive expands, it supplies additional momentum to attract greater opportunities. Generate energy reserves with advice from Archangel Michael. His powerful persona is impressive and he emanates strength. This Archangel approaches, holding a shiny breastplate made of pure silver. He places the *Armor of Power* over your chest, fortifying it with energy from his hand. Strength begins to course through your body as a power surge. Keep the breastplate on for an entire day, being aware of the extra power it creates. This angel will remain at close range while you wear the breastplate. In the evening, hand it back to Archangel Michael. He can leave now, knowing that you have constructive energy for activities requiring perseverance and phenomenal strength.

Dosage: In the morning, or as desired.

Preventive Medicine

Three remedies, two times a week
Two affirmations, four times a week

Prosperity Questions

Do angels intervene with people's health?
A goal for Guardian Angels is to help people generate energy flow for mental and physical well-being. They know that people have a greater zest for life, becoming vibrant and energized, when angels are invited to participate. Angels are happy to motivate individuals to achieve and then maintain optimum health.

Angel Specialist: Peter, Angel of Health

Primary Remedy: *Vitality Plus*

Can angels help people maintain their youth?
Angels are not able to provide the fountain of youth; however, they can supply guidance for living a more youthful life. Those who are invested in remaining energetic and vital stand a greater chance of preserving their youthful qualities. Individuals appear younger and look better when they are enthusiastic.

Angel Specialist: Esther, Angel of Vitality

Primary Remedy: *Cardio Dance*

Second Opinion

Christiana Cagnoni—*Master Shiatsu therapist/Chinese medicine practitioner. Chi-Lel/Qigong instructor. Founder: Matter of Flax, specializing in gluten-free, organic raw food.*

Health-conscious people initiate an ongoing relationship with their bodies, listening when their bodies speak to them. A person's body believes what it hears and will greatly benefit from receiving praise and positive reinforcement. Connecting to one's spirit is crucial. A spiritual connection is vital to people's bodies. It is as important as air, food, water, and exercise. When individuals live spiritual lives, they amass additional *Chi* or life force energy. Conscious breathing collects *Chi* and then allocates it for superior flow. Spiritual people create a reservoir of *Chi* energy. They use this energy for achieving peak performance in their activities. Enlightened individuals strive to maintain a high level of energy flow.

Keywords: Praise. Connect. Flow.

Miracle Story

Healing with Angels

At nine years old, Pedro was visited by an angel he named Samuel. Years later, in honor of that occasion, he planted a small garden in the yard behind his house. The garden led to his second encounter, for which Pedro is eternally grateful.

Working with a landscaping company requires stamina, agility, and endurance. Lifting and carrying flowers and pushing wheelbarrows full of dirt takes energy. While I was working one day, I tripped over a rake and twisted my left leg. Over time, it became stiff and sore. I found it difficult to stand and walk. Even shifting my weight to get in and out of bed was difficult and awkward.

For years, I tried doctors, acupuncture, chiropractic treatment, and physical therapy. Then I just gave up. In the spring, I planted a garden in my yard and added an angel statue. Looking at the statue from my window one day, I prayed for help.

That night, I woke up to someone trying to adjust my left leg. Three voices were discussing how to fix my leg, simultaneously pushing and pulling it. To my great amazement, the voices belonged to angels who looked transparent and were actually glowing. After the three had completed working on me, they floated off. My leg was healed—I could walk again! I am grateful to Samuel and the therapeutic garden angel who heard my prayer and responded.

Affirmations

I am proficient at prioritizing.

I have a well-organized home.

I am cleaning out any clutter.

I have a clean, orderly office.

I am happy to be responsible.

8
Organization

CONSULTATION

The judicious use of resources in conjunction with a viable plan to achieve objectives ultimately improves productivity. The goal of completing tasks and projects can be attained through systematic planning. A foundation for prosperity comes with solid organizational skills. Success necessitates perseverance and peak performance.

—JASON, ANGEL OF ORGANIZATION

Angel Specialists

Michael	Archangel
Cornell	Angel of Decisions
Courtney	Angel of Responsibility
George	Angel of Success
Mariann	Angel of Efficiency
Maureen	Angel of Time
Nancy	Angel of Productivity
Perrie	Angel of Music
Robert	Angel of Balance
Sally	Angel of Perseverance
Victoria	Angel of Guidance

CASE STUDY—News to Report

After identifying her life's purpose as being a writer, Charlotte had begun studying journalism. She remained optimistic as obstacles surfaced.

In my twenties, I was a college student with aspirations of becoming a writer. Although I worked hard to progress in most areas of my life, something new always seemed to get in the way of success. I kept missing the mark in terms of my career goals. My five-year relationship had not worked out, and I was overwhelmed with money issues. It became my responsibility to pay for college. Life was complicated. A writing career seemed impossible.

Working with The Angel Lady and practicing remedies changed my perspective. *Delegating to Angels* made school projects simpler and using *Baroque Beat* meant better concentration.

Within months, life started to turn around. For the first time, I became optimistic. I ended my relationship that was not working, as Jay entered my life. He is phenomenal and a person with a lifestyle better suited to mine. This term my grades were higher, allowing extra free time. Finances even improved after I landed a position with a substantial salary. I am excited to be working as a writer. Life has picked up, and many dreams are coming true.

Charlotte's Steps to Success

The path to success constantly offers opportunities to prove how much you want to reach your goals. A new perspective means that anything is possible with an open mind.

Remedies

Baroque Beat

Being well organized requires intention, concentration, motivation, and action. Make orderliness a priority for each aspect of your life. Listen to Baroque music in the background to create fresh ideas to organize thoughts. The tempo of each song synchronizes the music with the human brain. Imagine Perrie, Angel of Music, standing in front of you. He is an extraordinarily talented angel with an ear for music. Perrie begins to tap his wing tip to the beat. Start to tap your ring finger along with this angel for at least ten seconds. Switching to your right hand, tap to the rhythm, using your same finger. The true ability to focus has been enhanced. Return to the work at hand with a renewed attentiveness and finish the project. Perrie stays to enjoy the music.

Dosage: After breakfast, or as desired.

Three by Twelve

Gaining reassurance aids individuals in the process of making wise decisions. Clear thinking creates the ideal environment for various decision-making. Invite two proficient and adept angels to provide support and clarity as you ponder a situation. The first to appear is Sally, Angel of Perseverance. The second one is Victoria, Angel of Guidance. In unison, they recommend that, before making a major decision, you ask "How will the situation affect my life in the next twelve hours? How will the decision change my life throughout the next twelve weeks? How will this impact my life in the next twelve years?" After answering these three questions, you will know what action to take. Sally and Victoria offer their guidance before the two angels depart.

Dosage: As desired, for making decisions.

Taking Inventory

The primary characteristics of organized individuals are efficiency, promptness, reliability, and focus. With these traits, success will be easier to achieve. For this remedy, take inventory of your inherent attributes or abilities. Do they comprise the primary characteristics of an organized individual? Call on Robert, Angel of Balance, who has dark hair and blue eyes. He seems stable and steady. Robert's goal is to show you how to exhibit these qualities. If you possessed all four of the traits, would your life be different? Consider if your efficiency might improve. Begin to implement varied new ways to be productive. Visualize the faces and the reactions of family and friends as your life advances. Robert salutes your progress as he takes his leave.

Dosage: Three times a week.

Time Prosperity

Meeting an important deadline or organizing a large project can be accomplished through efficient time management. Take advantage of "Angelic Time" to reach a higher level of productivity. To begin using this basic remedy, call on Maureen, Angel of Time, with her raven-black hair and brown eyes. She helps you imagine your chest expanding approximately six inches on either side. Keep your body in this expanded state, holding extra space, until your work project is completed for the day. This enlarged capacity provides you with additional time to undertake extraordinary projects or multifaceted tasks. Maureen reminds you to return your chest to its normal size and shape when the project is completed. She departs after offering to return for your next complex endeavor.

Dosage: As required, for additional time.

Piece by Piece

Everyday responsibilities present circumstances that can be tackled with ease. Make tasks or projects effortless and less overwhelming by utilizing this remedy. Jason, the methodical and powerful Angel of Organization, stands before you with his broad shoulders. Draw a circle, representing a pie, and divide it into six slices. Label each of the slices with the necessary tasks. Highlight the piece requiring immediate attention. Place the five remaining wedges in the order of their importance. List the actions essential for completing tasks and projects. Address each action with a well-organized approach. Appreciate Jason's guidance while you finish one portion at a time. Savor each "bite" for its sweet taste of victory. Jason will applaud your success and offer his heartfelt praise.

Dosage: Each day, to prioritize.

Skyscraper Art

Procrastination is extremely difficult to overcome for most people. Putting off a task or delaying the start of a project is an avoidance mechanism. Ask Courtney, Angel of Responsibility, for assistance. A compassionate angel with brown hair and blue eyes, her precise manner is impressive. You feel very safe in her presence. Courtney suggests: "First, make a list of what has to be done. Second, draw a skyscraper. The building should have one floor for each task. Color it brightly and include a sun-filled sky." She encourages you to get started. After finishing each task and breathing a sigh of relief, tear off one floor of the skyscraper. When you reach ground level, your tenacity receives lavish praise from Courtney. She commends you by enthusiastically saying "Well done!"

Dosage: Once a week, or as needed.

Delegating to Angels

When people are organized and possess a clear mind, they are free to become more engaged in activities that bring them happiness. It often seems impossible to do everything by yourself, so delegate to Jason, Angel of Organization. Although he is of medium build, his strong shoulders can bear the weight of many duties. To start, put your name on the left side of a sheet of paper. Write Jason's name on the right. List tasks you can handle easily on the left and assign the others to Jason. Next, determine your plan of action. He will be of help in prioritizing and finishing tasks or projects. Jason enables you to complete duties rapidly because his energy reinforces yours. Extra time that is available can be used to pursue enjoyable activities. For fun, take Jason along.

Dosage: Once each day, or when desired.

Three in a Row

Maintaining balance while involved in organizing tasks or projects is a feat to admire. Under any type of circumstance, composure is a valuable asset. For the technique, two impressive angels stand by to be of assistance. Seek their advice before beginning organizational projects. Nancy, Angel of Productivity, conveys efficiency. Sally is the Angel of Perseverance. Her blue eyes exude intelligence. These two smart angels describe the technique: "Before, during, and after a project that requires concentration, draw three equidistant lines on a white sheet of paper. These lines are drawn the same distance apart and matched perfectly in length. Repeat each set three times." Now that you have regained focus, all prospects look bright. These angels reappear for organizing ventures.

Dosage: When useful; to regain balance.

Keep or Toss

Organization allows for better energy flow and subsequently helps people be productive. Removing clutter assists in regaining a sense of equilibrium. Summon Cornell, Angel of Decisions, with his tall stature, sandy brown hair, and bright blue discerning eyes, to help in organizing a room. Both of you place everything in three cartons labeled KEEP, TOSS, and MAYBE. Ask yourself, "Do I have a purpose for this item? Will I use this ever again?" Select the right box. Items in the KEEP box will eventually make their way back into the room. All items for the TOSS box will be thrown away or donated. Items in the MAYBE box will be sorted one more time. The items going back into the room have their specific place. Cornell leaves, sharing your enthusiastic feeling of accomplishment.

Dosage: Once a month, or as needed.

Preventive Medicine

Four remedies, two times a week
Three affirmations, four times a week

Prosperity Questions

Can angels initiate increased productivity?
Angels have unlimited resources available to help individuals work toward developing motivation for organizational projects. This can ease the completion of any task at hand. They provide constructive ideas that inspire individuals to become efficient. When angels are in attendance, productivity increases.

Angel Specialist: Nancy, Angel of Productivity

Primary Remedy: *Delegating to Angels*

Does angelic intervention ease responsibility?
As valuable companions, angels are thrilled to provide the tools to make responsibilities more manageable. They will bear the weight of tasks, lightening the load. Individuals become motivated as they share responsibilities with their angelic support system. Teamwork makes completing projects much easier.

Angel Specialist: Jason Angel of Organization

Primary Remedy: *Piece by Piece*

Second Opinion

Rita Emmet—*Business consultant, motivational speaker, seminar facilitator, and teacher. Author of* The Procrastinator's Handbook. *Presents course covering organizational skills.*

One interesting secret to organization or time management is that busy people really do have a choice: they can say "no." When they are considering a new project, people should weigh the importance of each request. Realize that costly decisions call for more thought, energy, and elbow grease. It is best to allow extra time—as well as to allocate extra funds—for larger projects. Every day, people need to prioritize goals and commit to objectives to generate prosperity. It also helps to find humor in all situations. Bringing levity as well as laughter into one's organizational activities will lighten the load. The achievements garnered from living an orderly life, filled with humor, will quickly lead to self-empowerment.

Keywords: Organization. Goals. Humor.

Miracle Story

Blinked to Safety

Josephine and her family were traveling through the Midwest after having spent the holidays with their relatives. The trip was difficult enough entertaining small children, and then a snowstorm became a worrisome factor. Angels to the rescue!

The snowstorm had escalated to blizzard conditions. All visibility became impaired, which made driving unsafe. Tim could not find a cleared exit, so he kept on driving.

While Tim focused on the road, four red, blinking taillights shone in the distance, so he reduced his speed. Even though he could not see the car in front of him, he kept his eyes on the red taillights, which shone brightly through all the heavy snow. Then our car hit a massive patch of ice and began to drift. Luckily, Tim was able to keep the car under control as he had slowed down. The lights immediately disappeared in the blowing snow.

Five minutes later, the same red blinking taillights reappeared in the distance. Cautiously, Tim decreased our speed. He hit another patch of ice, but still managed to keep control of the car. The lights disappeared again. Throughout the trip, we never spotted any other vehicle on the road in front of us. Later, very happy to be home, I figured it out. Our Guardian Angels were on the road, and they had "blinked" us to safety mile by mile.

Affirmations

I am affluent and prosperous.

I have unlimited funds to use.

I am exceedingly resourceful.

I have wealth and abundance.

I am making a steady income.

9
Finances

CONSULTATION

Prosperity in the form of abundance creates an atmosphere of richness in life. Individuals will flourish with a continual influx of funds and revenue flow available for investment in personal or professional endeavors. Financial independence in conjunction with the other aspects of prosperity provides the freedom to pursue dreams.

—JEREMIAH, ANGEL OF FINANCIAL SECURITY

Angel Specialists

Uriel	Archangel
Alan	Angel of Investments
Evelyn	Angel of Manifesting
Jacob	Angel of Education
Katrina	Angel of Prosperity
Laramie	Angel of Discovery
Lucian	Angel of Resources
Theresa	Angel of Empowerment
Timothy	Angel of Good Fortune
Trevor	Angel of Stocks
Tyler	Angel of Abundance

CASE STUDY—Moving on Up

Making it in through the day with three teenage children kept Beth busy. Her career as a journalist was not financially feasible for her family.

I believe in angels. My assignment for a newspaper fortified my faith. I interviewed The Angel Lady, who clearly related guidance from the Guardian Angels. As a single mom with three children, paying daily attention to finances was more than important. It made perfect sense that a smart strategy would be to apply *Laws for Life,* especially my favorite one, Law of Attraction. My ideal plan was to use this technique often throughout each day.

Achieving career goals was also a priority. I prayed for the financial success necessary to support my family. After using The Angel Lady's techniques, an associate offered me a job at her company. This new salary represented a major jump—my income increased sevenfold! I was now able to better provide for my teenagers.

After achieving success and financial security, I began the search for my soulmate. My daily ritual became asking the "love" angels to find my ideal man. Mark, a well-known TV personality, remembered me from an interview. After a brief courtship, he professed his love, and we were married. My family now has true joy.

Beth's Steps to Success

Make it your intention to succeed, and it will happen. Believe that angels are prepared to help and set your goals high. Trust in angels to supply—in perfect form—what you desire.

Remedies
Wealth Affirmation

Affirming wealth is a surefire way to realize prosperity and amass a fortune. An affluent lifestyle opens numerous doors and produces an opportunity to make a difference in other people's lives. Calling upon Evelyn, Angel of Manifesting, ensures that you are setting up a consistent—as well as ample—supply of funds. Evelyn's manner indicates a bright, sophisticated angel. She suggests: "Tap on both sides of your head in the temple area, and simultaneously repeat a potent affirmation: *'I give myself permission to be wealthy!'*" Use this powerful remedy often while picturing yourself living the life of an exuberant, happy, and wealthy person. Think of the feelings of joy that can come with financial independence. Evelyn asks to be included in future prosperous events.

Dosage: Throughout the day for prosperity.

Money Magnet

A continuous influx of capital creates momentum for a higher level of freedom. To increase funds and amass wealth, use this technique with Tyler, Angel of Abundance. You note his genuinely magnetic personality and charismatic air. He is a key player for this exercise. Tyler extends his right hand, sending out a magnetic beam. Feel its intensity. The beam permeates your body, mind, and spirit. Realize your newfound ability to attract unlimited wealth. Tyler advocates repeating this powerful affirmation: *I am a Mighty Money Magnet!* State it with deliberate enthusiasm as you picture currency coming toward you from every direction. Reach out and catch the cash that sparks financial growth and independence. Before the angel leaves, he applauds your progress.

Dosage: Throughout the day, for increased funds.

Dollar Sign

Attract supplemental funds to facilitate economic success and good fortune. This becomes an easy remedy to experience financial gain. Take the index finger of your dominant hand to draw small dollar signs in the air directly in front of you. Really concentrate on these symbols, drawing them larger and larger until your entire body is a part of the motion. Repeat the exercise seven times, always starting with a small dollar sign. Designating a purpose for the funds makes the money multiply faster. Summon Evelyn, Angel of Manifesting, a statuesque angel who loves to draw. She faces you, and together you draw dollar signs over and over again. This angel will provide opportunities for increasing prosperity. Evelyn wants to be invited each time dollar signs are being drawn.

Dosage: As desired, for fast cash.

Four Winds

Accelerate prosperity by gaining the capability to manifest or make dreams a reality. This can generate monumental rewards. Welcome Lucian, Angel of Resources. He is on hand to practice this remedy. His light-colored hair accentuates his brilliant blue eyes. Visualize Lucian standing by your side in a park-like area surrounded by oak trees. Notice the grass, gentle breeze, and stately trees with foliage rustling in the wind. Lucian teaches you how to establish multiple sources of income. Face forward; picture an income stream that is blowing toward you. Extend your arms and draw it in. Now invite this income stream to remain in your body. Repeat this process in all four directions. Lucian recognizes that the four winds blowing create prosperity.

Dosage: Twice a day, morning and evening.

Stacking Cash

Guardian Angels know that people can manifest as much money as their minds and bodies will accept. This financial remedy prepares people to receive money. Notice Timothy, Angel of Good Fortune, who stands tall and strong. The angel presents you with numerous handfuls of cash. Every piece of currency will be a $50 or $100 bill. Start stacking these bills next to you. Reach out for more. Timothy quickly replenishes your supply each time your hand extends out to him. When the cash is overflowing, Timothy hands you a golden key to open a "safe" in the center of your body. Place the money in the safe. Feel the excitement of having discretionary funds to enjoy each day. Offer thanks to Timothy for handing you the golden key to your fortune.

Dosage: Once a day, in the morning.

Play Money

Enjoying being wealthy can mean experiencing a genuine sense of well-being. Become accustomed to money in larger quantities, and greater amounts of cash will begin to enter your life. Being at ease with amassing large sums is a signal to Tyler, Angel of Abundance, that he can supply financial blessings. Tyler, tall and muscular, has a thought. He intimates: "I have a secret for you. Keep play-money in your wallet or purse." Visualize being confident and successful. Enjoy each moment. When you see or touch this "pretend cash," it demonstrates to all of the angels your ability to accept abundance. Tyler takes this one step further by saying, "Spread your wealth by sharing the phenomenal secret with others you care about and who hold a very special place in your heart."

Dosage: As desired, for extra cash.

Bank Rolls

Individuals can allow angelic power to elevate their prosperity and provide greater abundance. This can be accomplished by becoming accustomed to finding money. Laramie, Angel of Discovery, wants to participate in this remedy. This financially savvy angel, with his dark brown hair and sparkling blue eyes, leads you on your journey of discovery. To start, have forty one-dollar bills. Take about seven singles, roll them together, and secure each roll with a rubber band. Put these rolls in drawers, cabinets, pockets, your car, your office, or wherever you will notice them every day. Laramie enjoys your elated reaction when you locate a part of this stash. Find currency in familiar places to "think rich." Laramie is considering an option to "bankroll" your financial venture.

Dosage: Whenever additional cash is desired.

Plug the Drain

When individuals have expenditures that far exceed incomes, there is a continual drain on revenue. Call on a "money" angel to fix the predicament. Jeremiah, Angel of Financial Security, is visible with his expansive golden wings. He instructs you to start by imagining a grand old-fashioned bathtub filled to the top with cash belonging to you. Jeremiah puts a large plug in the drain. He prevents a tubful of money from "going down the drain." The financial angel reveals a visualization. Imagine yourself standing near a fountain shooting streams of water high in the air. Observe the arc of the spray, while recognizing that *the fountain symbolizes your money supply* being replenished. Enjoy a perpetual cash flow and a steady income. You and Jeremiah will be rejoicing forever.

Dosage: Once a day, or as needed.

Easy Money

Prosperity-minded individuals seek places to find additional funds. Tremendous opportunities can present themselves in exceptional ways. The remedy works to accumulate monies for building assets. Imagine being seated at a desk. Lucian, Angel of Resources, enters with fifteen moneybags brimming with cash. While he pours them on the desk one at a time, watch the mountain of money growing. Engage your senses. Feel the texture of the currency. Capture this moment by locking it into your mind as a "snapshot." Realize how easy it will be to have wealth as a part of your life. Lucian advises: "Invest the money judiciously. Watch the capital grow throughout the coming years." Before the Angel of Resources parts company, he predicts: "Easy Money is on its way!"

Dosage: Twice a day, morning and evening.

Preventive Medicine

Two remedies, three times a week
Three affirmations, four times a week

Prosperity Questions

How do angels impact financial security?

Angels consider prosperity to be of major importance for everyone. They generate abundant funds for people, helping them fulfill their destinies and enjoy life. Individuals who achieve financial security find it easier to be spontaneous in pursuing opportunities or other creative endeavors in their daily lives.

Angel Specialist: Jeremiah, Angel of Financial Security

Primary Remedy: *Four Winds*

Do angels intervene in financial endeavors?

Many aspects of individuals' financial matters benefit from angelic guidance. They provide support when planning budgets, managing accounts, and generating income. Handling all fiscal investments is seamless when angels are involved. Guardian Angels happily assist people with the financial aspects of life.

Angel Specialist: Timothy, Angel of Good Fortune

Primary Remedy: *Money Magnet*

Second Opinion

Portia Carmichael—*Founder of Smith/Carmichael Financial, firm providing investments and mediation. Formerly a bilingual teacher and Instructor of Economics, Union College.*

Prosperity is a dynamic in which the aspects of life (family, career, finances, recreation, and relaxation) are appropriately balanced. As individuals sustain this equilibrium, a prosperous state of being is sustained. Empowered by this newfound stabilizing energy, people grow exponentially. Achieving balance is a process beginning with qualities such as perseverance, tenacity, and time management. All are required to build the foundation that allows individuals to have discretionary time and money. People should also be aware of their work ethics, along with how they expect to use income. Financially rewarding endeavors become more satisfying when money is being dispersed for the betterment of others.

Keywords: Balance. Tenacity. Integrity.

Miracle Story

You Can Bank on It

A twenty-year veteran of the police department, Mike was a month away from retirement. At that point, an angelic intervention would change his life. His wife Cheri recounted their amazing story to the audience at a seminar about angels.

Dispatch had put out an urgent bulletin: "Bank robbery in progress; single male, armed." First on the scene, my husband Mike spotted the getaway car from his cruiser. He radioed his location and looked up. Mike saw a man with an assault rifle. The suspect fired through the door, hitting Mike in the hip. He radioed "Officer down" and slid out the door and onto the ground. Then the robber ran around the cruiser, firing again at point blank range. Mike played dead. The thief took off on foot as a crowd began to gather.

Later, at the hospital, I prayed throughout the time Mike was in surgery. My family refused to believe me as I assured them that he would recover. Visiting Mike in the ICU, I saw a vision: in a huge stadium, the bleachers were filled with hundreds of cheering angels. A sense of peace washed over me when I came back to reality, and started to reach for Mike's hand.

After the vision, I knew Mike would fully recover. Two years have passed. My husband and I are assisting others by hosting presentations on the amazing healing powers of angels.

Affirmations

I am a very successful person.

I have honorable work ethics.

I am using professional skills.

I have an aptitude for service.

I am known for my creativity.

10

Success

CONSULTATION

Personal empowerment becomes a fundamental or crucial component in the quest for prosperity. Individuals who are successful experience a sense of personal satisfaction. Good fortune permeates every facet of their daily lives. A genuine measure of success is the contentment and fulfillment that is realized when individuals excel.

—GEORGE, ANGEL OF SUCCESS

Angel Specialists

Michael	**Archangel**
Cornell	Angel of Decisions
Cory	Angel of Careers
Darla	Angel of Enlightenment
Deborah	Angel of Interviewing
Jonathan	Angel of Business
Katrina	Angel of Prosperity
Lucian	Angel of Resources
Patrick	Angel of Sports
Rebecca	Angel of Confidence
Samuel	Angel of Excellence

CASE STUDY—Success in the City

Open to all possibilities, James counted on his angels for assistance. He created everyday miracles while traveling on the fast track to success.

After I had finished graduate school, I was ready to find the right job. Discovering *Angel First Aid* inspired me to begin each day with remedies. *Interview Preview* and my favorite one, *Confidence Builder,* expanded my horizons. Practice is important, so I did not miss a day.

My headhunter set up an interview in Los Angeles with the manager of a company that had become my first choice. As I drove through downtown to get to my interview, I was nervous about my ability to respond to questions. However, as the skyline came into view, my evident pressing problem became rush hour! The bumper-to-bumper traffic changed my focus. My interview started in forty-five minutes, and it was an hour away. Quickly, I called for Maureen, Angel of Time, to clear traffic. The effect was instantaneous. Cars deliberately avoided my lane. What a miracle! I made it in thirty minutes with time to spare.

The interview went fantastically, and I was hired on the spot. Today, my career remains successful. The Angels keep me busy with exciting opportunities, and I thank them each day—especially Angel Maureen.

James's Steps to Success

Allow yourself to be open to guidance, direction, and wisdom from Guardian Angels. Put your trust in them to deliver superior results for every situation and circumstance.

Remedies

Ready, Set, Goals!

Regular use of affirmations enables people to manifest their goals. Declarative statements, verbalized and written correctly, accelerate the accomplishment of vital goals. Darla, Angel of Enlightenment, enters and recommends using this remedy. Although Darla's wings are immense, they do not distract from her flowing, orchid-colored gown. Following this angel's lead, take one sheet of unlined paper and write down any objectives you want to attain. Make sure every goal is written as an affirmation. These statements begin with *I am* ___ or *I have* ___. Be specific, to achieve the desired result. For example, *I have my career on track to success.* Darla celebrates your advancement. Both of you have been enriched. She gracefully flies off.

Dosage: Once a day, after breakfast.

Yes or No

Making solid decisions is paramount when considering a change in careers. While conducting a job search, formulate major decisions carefully. To determine the career that best incorporates a purpose in life, use this exercise: Envision twelve angels in attendance. Next, put the fingertips of both hands in the center of your chest, on your breastbone. Choose a career and make a straightforward statement to see if this position is the most suitable. Say, "A job as a computer programmer is the best choice for me." If your body leans forward, the answer is yes. If it moves backward, select another option. The body's innate intelligence will provide answers to questions in any area of life. Angels recommend using Yes or No as a guidance tool for decisions in life.

Dosage: As desired, for decision-making.

Confidence Builder

When individuals fortify physical energy, they generate confidence to meet fascinating people. Activating acupressure points improves energy flow. Practice this remedy when it is advantageous to make an impression. Rebecca, Angel of Confidence, is waiting nearby to assist. With your dominant hand, rub across the bottom of your rib cage five times. One back-and-forth movement counts as one time. Cross both arms over your chest, grasping the upper arm below the shoulders, and rub up and down five times. Next, place both hands on the outside of each thigh, apply slight pressure, and slide up and down, hip to knee, five times. Note how much straighter you stand. Rebecca knows for a fact that you will make a truly good impression on everyone.

Dosage: Twice a day, or for a boost.

Interview Preview

Consulting with Guardian Angels can assist in building confidence, especially in situations relating to career advancement. Before the job interview, perform this effective remedy. Begin by visualizing yourself walking down a theater aisle toward a grand stage. Climb the seven stairs onto the large platform, where four Archangels are waiting, standing in a semicircle. They are ready to put a crimson ribbon holding a gold medal around your neck. It is the time to feel victorious and proud to be recognized for all of your achievements. For one minute, hold the exhilaration of being appreciated for your endeavors. Next, exit the stage, passing the audience as you depart. Smile while each person extends congratulations. The angels have offered their reward. You are a winner!

Dosage: Three times a week, or before an interview.

Career Bliss

Manifesting professional goals becomes necessary when seeking a rewarding career. This creates a road map to success in life. Select Cory, Angel of Careers, as a guide for this exciting adventure. His notable strength surrounds you with a tremendous sense of safety for the journey. Visualize landing the perfect job. Imagine standing in the basket of a hot-air balloon that sets down beside the building where your new job is located. Start looking around. Observe each detail related to the position: personalities of all of your colleagues, general policies, the working environment, and how management operates. Picture your new office with its color, location, windows, furnishings, and decor. When complete, Cory escorts you back to the balloon and navigates the wonderous trip home.

Dosage: As required, or until employed.

Steps to Success

Working for a large corporation can be exceptionally invigorating. The doors of opportunity can open through multiple tiers. Ascend the ladder of success by asking yourself two questions: What is the highest level I can achieve? How do I get there? To accomplish this remedy, think of yourself waiting at the bottom of a staircase, ready to climb to the top. Ask Samuel, Angel of Excellence, to accompany you on this exciting journey. Each step taken represents one tier of power within the company. Ascending the long staircase, Samuel is positive and relishes the climb. His participation strengthens your resolve to keep climbing. Reaching the top, rejoice. You have made it this far. Samuel waits with pride to escort you down the staircase and applaud your achievements.

Dosage: Twice a week, for greater success.

Instant Replay

Visualizing athletic triumphs is the secret to making them a reality. The subconscious mind does not differentiate between an activity that is being performed and one that is visualized. "Practice makes perfect" in either form. Patrick, Angel of Sports, joins your team to assist with preparations for a big game. This handsome angel, with his athletic build, declares, "Begin by envisioning each step you will take to win." Be meticulous, and pinpoint motions and actions that will improve your performance. Replay all parts of the routine until it is flawless. Imagine yourself exulting in the thrill of victory! Hold this high level of enthusiasm for one minute. While participating in a sport, visualize Patrick actively cheering from the sidelines. He is one of your biggest fans.

Dosage: Three times a day, before a game.

King of the Mountain

Prosperity becomes attainable if individuals reproduce many of the achievements and accomplishments that have proven successful in their lives. Prepare yourself to scale a massive mountain of success. Wearing appropriate gear makes this journey realistic. With every step, you are a more skilled, more competent climber able to reach the top. At the summit, thank the angels, consultants, and business associates who have acted as your mentors. Now it is the best time to acknowledge them. Recall all the benefits from their leadership. During your decent, express extreme gratitude for the many forms of guidance that have been available to you. Angels are proud to be part of the mentoring team. They will continue supporting actions that make you "King of the Mountain."

Dosage: Three times a week, for confidence.

Shower of Money

Inviting angelic encouragement leads to remarkable success in life. Accept the support from angels to achieve prosperity. To start, use this easy remedy, which is imaginatively set in a ticker-tape parade. Picture yourself seated on the back of a new red convertible next to George, Angel of Success. His golden locks and colorful green toga are sparkling in the sunlight. The convertible is surrounded. People are cheering and enthusiastic. Interspersed throughout this crowd, angels are thrilled and smiling with pride. You bask in the glory of thousands of $100 bills showering down from above. Welcome all the riches that are being lavishly bestowed upon you. At the end of the parade, give a triumphant wave to the crowd. Angels have left to gather additional "money" confetti for the next parade.

Dosage: Once a day, for prosperity.

Preventive Medicine

Two remedies, two times a week
Four affirmations, three times a week

Prosperity Questions

How do angels advance people's careers?
Prosperity-minded individuals can count on the angels for support. Whether it is encouragement throughout a job interview, guidance for navigating office politics, or assistance with a promotion, many angels are on duty to provide motivation. They inspire individuals to capitalize on their inherent talents.

Angel Specialist: Cory, Angel of Careers

Primary Remedy: *Steps to Success*

Can angels drive successful endeavors?
Angels are adept at steering applicants in search of employment to vocations that will match their skills. They provide advice, bolster confidence, and present exciting opportunities. Angelic guidance is genuinely beneficial and lucrative, stimulating candidates to obtain rewarding and profitable occupations.

Angel Specialist: George, Angel of Success

Primary Remedy: *Career Bliss*

Second Opinion

George Pradel—*Mayor of Naperville, Illinois. Police Department: "Officer Friendly." Advisory Board: DePaul University and DuPage County Police Association. Started Safety Town.*

Success in all aspects of life is best achieved by putting others first and letting them grow. Giving is its own reward. Communication becomes essential. People must strive to be open and up front with any personal expectations before they take action. This can create a smoother, more beneficial outcome. Teamwork remains important in advancing various goals of a community and its quality of life. If all individuals provide key ideas and volunteer to implement them, the entire community benefits. When citizens reach out and share their talents and abilities, those living in the town prosper. Success can definitely be accomplished when Guardian Angels are invited to participate and be part of the team.

Keywords: Teamwork. Community. Advancement.

Miracle Story

The Power of Intention

Kathleen, in her forties and a stay-at-home mom, had lost her dear husband early in their marriage. As a widow, she was raising four children on a tight budget. She called upon the angels for support. It seemed like her only hope at the time.

The loss of my husband after only ten years of marriage meant that I would have to return to work and support my four children. I was unclear about what occupation to pursue. One night, an angel appeared in my dream. He advised, "Go to nursing school." Later, with an RN degree, my budget was still tight.

Working long hours and constantly trying to make ends meet, I often asked my angels for a way to increase my income. One night in another vivid dream, an angel pointed to a book about visualizations. Lo and behold, I found it at the library the next day. The method I chose required imagining a specific amount of money. A sum of $400,000 came to me: $100,000 per child. I began to practice this visualization technique on a daily basis.

A year later, a private investigator called. I thought that he was kidding when he said that I had inherited a substantial amount of money. I ignored the call. On the following day, he came to my house and told me about an aunt that I had never met. She had left me $400,000. Angels were right on the money!

Affirmations

I am a professional executive.

I have a prosperous company.

I am sharing leadership skills.

I have created a strategic plan.

I am an adept business leader.

11

Business

CONSULTATION

Successful entrepreneurs create a vision and a plan for the advancement of their companies. Executives that strive for excellence exercise their insight and intuition to manifest the effective implementation of various business strategies. Raising the bottom line through attaining goals will ensure profitability in business ventures.

—JONATHAN, ANGEL OF BUSINESS

Angel Specialists

Gabriel	Archangel
Christopher	Angel of Opportunity
David	Angel of Camaraderie
Deborah	Angel of Interviewing
Jason	Angel of Organization
Jordan	Angel of Teamwork
Leslie	Angel of Diplomacy
Loretta	Angel of New Enterprise
Marcus	Angel of Sales
Nancy	Angel of Productivity
Randolph	Angel of Expansion

CASE STUDY—Finding the Right Path

Although this young woman had tasted success at an early age, she felt something was still missing. Many pathways led Donna to fulfillment.

To make a difference in the world, I became a lawyer and a CPA. However, attaining a high level of success by the age of thirty does not necessarily correspond to making a great contribution to the world. Therefore, searching for the lack of purpose in my life compelled me to identify my mission. My goal was to research varied resources and determine my divine purpose in life.

Soon I read about Angel First Aid Techniques. Book in hand, I started with *Angel Scrapbook*, as it felt most logical. While performing the technique, I recalled a scene where I protected one of my young playmates from a bully. What a moment! My purpose was to champion the rights of people who really needed a good defense. This dose of reality helped my career.

Identifying my purpose ignited my passion to make a real difference. I pondered advice from Archangel Michael. He helped me to seek out and litigate for the disadvantaged. Now I advocate for people's rights for fair treatment. I have become their best warrior in both financial and legal arenas, where I excel.

Donna's Steps to Success

Look through the glasses of integrity and truth. Focus on a strategy and persevere, no matter what happens. Pursue the career path that can truly facilitate your life's purpose.

Remedies

Vision Statement

The most successful corporations have specific mission statements. Effective businesses move a step further, creating a realistic vision statement. This is a plan representing your vision for the future of the corporation. Formulate a strategic pathway, and employ angels as advisers. Their direct assistance contributes to the growth of the organization. Together, compose affirmations that define plans for your business's long-term development. Examples of affirmations to use: *I have a successful business plan in place. I am developing the strategies essential to meet the vision statement. I am fulfilling the company's mission.* Repeat them aloud five times a day. This is the perfect signal to notify the angels of your intention to solidify a profitable business.

Dosage: Once a day, in the morning.

Painting for Progress

Entrepreneurs solicit guidance from angels to establish a visionary concept. Astute leaders recognize that to solidly impact the bottom line, a business plan is mandatory. To start this technique, visualize a large golden frame of a painting representing your five-year plan. Paint a picture of how the company will thrive within the next five years. Include the new mission and vision statements, highlighting supporting goals. Emphasize bright, vibrant colors as you meander through offices and note exceptional floor plans. Listen for phones ringing, employees working with customers, and pitches from your jubilant sales force guided by Marcus, Angel of Sales. Concentrate for one minute on this profitable scene. Angels use the artwork to help propel your instantaneous success.

Dosage: Twice a day, for increased sales.

Meeting an Angel

Viable connections are essential to furthering a professional career. Networking is the path to developing the playing field to grow your business. Employ this remedy to generate many profitable business contacts. Playing the role of an entrepreneur at a networking event, you arrive feeling dynamic and energized. In the supporting role is Loretta, Angel of New Enterprise. Staying nearby, she encourages you to network with attendees. People are fascinated as they listen intently to all of your intriguing ideas and creative strategies. Keep communicating; "work the room," gathering confidence with every viable new contact. Enjoy the thrill of others seeking your business knowledge and advice. After your latest connections are solidified, Loretta takes her briefcase and flies off.

Dosage: Three times a week, or before networking.

Angelic Voice Mail

Successful professionals seek the advice of mentors to become top performers. Fortunately, angelic wisdom can be only a phone call away. Jonathan, Angel of Business, with his deep baritone voice, is waiting for your call. Dial his direct line, note his greeting, and hear harp music in the background. After the beep, leave a request and listen for a response. His reply may not be immediate. Your answer will not always come from Jonathan personally. Watch for unusual events that convey a message: in a song, from a friend, or through a familiar incident. Requests left on Jonathan's voice mail just before midnight will be returned the following morning. Jonathan checks his messages often. Rest assured; he will get back to you in some understandable way.

Dosage: Four times a week, or as desired.

Expand Your Territory

Consistent growth is a necessary aspect in each long-term business strategy. Create the plan to target and secure a loyal customer base. Ask Randolph, Angel of Expansion, for his ideas and contributions for enlarging your territory. Visualize a map, including the specific geographical area you would like to cover. Take a blue marker and outline the borders that determine the corporation's vision for the future. To highlight the region for expansion, insert blue pushpins. Each pushpin represents a viable connection and customer. Allow the excitement of overwhelming success to encompass your being. Now all industrious efforts will create profitable, productive sales. Establishing new parameters lets angels recognize exactly where to target their blessings most effectively.

Dosage: Once a day, in the morning.

Business Honors

Executives and employees will be validated when efforts are being rewarded. Recognition energizes everyone's spirits and encourages their constant participation. Celebrate your contributions with this exhilarating remedy. In the scenario, you are accepting the coveted Customer Service Award from industry peers. Standing close by is Deborah, Angel of Interviewing. Her distinguished appearance and striking look of self-confidence are impressive. The angel requests that you reveal a few beneficial tips used to ensure success. Your reply: "Become a passionate listener, make customer satisfaction a priority, and offer quality products." As the ceremony comes to an end, the audience claps and Deborah presents a plaque and a sizable check.

Dosage: Three times a week.

Morale Booster

When employees' input is valued, they eagerly make contributions toward common goals. Create excitement that is contagious among the team, enabling a free flow of ingenious ideas. For the technique, you become the coordinator of a large company picnic. This event brings together members of the corporation from across the globe. Upper management anticipates complete success. Visualize David, Angel of Camaraderie, leaning against a tree as he offers advice on building a solid foundation of honesty and integrity. Instruct all the employees to brainstorm ideas and submit them for a review. Each executive committee member endorses these results and stamps his seal of approval. David extols your team's superb performance, and everyone quickly returns to the picnic.

Dosage: Every other day, for better morale.

Sales for Success

Financial growth becomes accelerated through excellent marketing of sales concepts. The secret of success is in the superb presentation of a product. Visualize a scenario in which Marcus, Angel of Sales, is a confident manager presenting a seminar entitled "Meeting and Exceeding Quotas." The energy level in the room heightens during his pep talk. Procedures will be included that detail ways to expand customer satisfaction. Marcus discusses identifying and selecting a target market for advertising purposes. Reflect on points presented and how they can be implemented to generate product interest and increased revenue. Marcus pinpoints the advantages of associating with the Angelic Realm. After the seminar is concluded, try out your tools for success.

Dosage: Three times a week, for making quotas.

Team Strategy

Teamwork is the pivotal requirement necessary for an organization to flourish. It requires uniting singular efforts toward one common purpose. Jordan, Angel of Teamwork, strong and compassionate, is a consultant. The two of you are at a construction site to conduct a meeting. Imaginary blueprints represent plans for attaining specific objectives. Work together with this crew to develop a strategy that will bring the project to fruition. Listen as the crew members offer innovative ideas and eagerly discuss their roles on this exceptional project. Team enthusiasm builds when the participants feel valued. They know that achievement of personal goals will also enable the company to prosper. With Jordan working alongside, finalize plans for the project's triumphant conclusion.

Dosage: Every other day, for teamwork.

Preventive Medicine

Two remedies, three times a week
Three affirmations, four times a week

Prosperity Questions

Can angels improve management skills?
Entrepreneurs thrive from angelic consultations that encourage the development of high-performance management teams. Executives who connect with angels recognize the fact that focus and clarity of thought enhances their management skills. Leaders are born when angels and professionals form a team.

Angel Specialist: Jordan, Angel of Teamwork

Primary Remedy: *Vision Statement*

How do angels support business ventures?
Angels back business owners in obtaining funds, hiring employees, and attracting customers. They assist during the process of forming new companies and in routine operations of established businesses. Angels infuse executives with the vision of excellence, the direction to succeed, and the power to prosper.

Angel Specialist: Jonathan, Angel of Business

Primary Remedy: *Expand Your Territory*

Second Opinion

Richard Green—*Retired president of Blistex, Inc. Past affiliations: Business Leaders for Excellence, Ethics, and Justice; Chairman of the Consumer Health Products Association.*

There is no one secret formula for becoming a success in business and life. Each situation that arises will have different components no matter how consistent they may seem. Stay open and aware of the potential for advancement. The main plan is to go with the flow of every opportunity. Take advantage of any educational prospect, learning as much as possible. Training oneself to approach life this way will increase knowledge and improve skills. With work habits, pay attention to punctuality, accuracy, and detail. Always go above and beyond what is expected. Concentrate on productivity as well as on the welfare of everyone concerned; customers and employees. Give it your all, and you will succeed!

Keywords: Education. Diligence. Discipline.

Miracle Story

Chairman of the Board

Steve, CEO of an international corporation, refers to his Guardian Angel in an unusual way. In this story he reveals the extraordinary gift of prophecy his Guardian Angel delivered through very bizarre circumstances on a chilly afternoon.

During childhood, the letters "CEO" would intrigue me. A joyful feeling was associated with them and resonated throughout my body. Seeing these initials made me laugh.

Later in my teens, I lacked ambition and had little interest in my future career. Walking home from school one blustery, cold day, I stepped into an old abandoned warehouse to warm up. Directly in front of me stood an unusually tall gray-haired bearded man wearing a white suit. To my surprise, he had wings!

Was my mind playing tricks on me? This kind man began to speak in clear tones. He described exactly how my future would evolve, even predicting an Ivy League college graduation. The angel said that I would become an entrepreneur and businessman. Suddenly, this man I later called "CEO" simply vanished.

The angel's predictions somehow transformed me from a teenager with little drive to becoming chairman of the board. Today, I recall the memories of childhood while I proudly share the acronym CEO with an executive Guardian Angel.

Affirmations

I have supreme spiritual love.

I am whole in body and spirit.

I have a full and peaceful life.

I am receiving universal love.

I have miracles and blessings.

12
Spirituality

CONSULTATION

Spirituality is the core of existence and a direct connection to inner peace. Individuals are linked to the richness of life through their beliefs and personal perceptions. Being united with spirit allows people to enjoy increased prosperity. This alignment contributes to individuals experiencing harmony and contentment in all aspects of life.

—DARLA, ANGEL OF ENLIGHTENMENT

Angel Specialists

Uriel	Archangel
Alicia	Angel of Serenity
Bradley	Angel of Purpose
Christine	Angel of Spontaneity
Josephine	Angel of Inner Peace
Leslie	Angel of Diplomacy
Paula	Angel of Energy
Ursula	Angel of Alignment
Valerie	Angel of Understanding
Victoria	Angel of Guidance
William	Angel of Peace

CASE STUDY—Starting Over

In an honest effort to bring more peace and prosperity into her life, Nora had to concentrate on simplifying her schedule. She wanted to succeed.

A woman of forty, I had experienced several successes, but I mostly faced challenges. My rewarding academic career was also problematic, and I was supporting two teenagers.

Although I had a PhD, it seemed impossible to secure a full-time position. As a professor, I drove from one campus to another—sometimes five a day. This was crucial for my many part-time jobs.

Everything seemed to be spiraling out of control. Then one night on the radio, I heard the voice of The Angel Lady. It felt like the angels' love was flowing from my car radio to my heart. It gave me hope. I contacted The Angel Lady and practiced the techniques in her books. My spirits high, my career began to soar.

I now have a full-time position and a short, enjoyable commute. This allows me additional time for my teenagers and eliminates my financial worries. My life has been truly blessed with happiness that I graciously share with others. I will forever be grateful to the angels for the love that caught my attention on the radio.

Nora's Steps to Success

Let angels guide you to hope and prosperity. Their special wisdom can enlighten your life. Believe in your abilities, but also have faith that angels will offer their love and guidance.

Remedies

Pathway to Peace

It is beneficial for individuals to enjoy some tranquil moments on a regular basis. The rewards show up in the well-being of both mind and body. Visualize a walk with William, Angel of Peace. A gentle, wise, caring angel, he suggests a walk on a winding path. Speaking clearly, William asks you, "If peace became the sole priority in your life, what would you do differently?" Take time to contemplate this profound question. Formulate your meaningful answer, and share your response with Angel William. Ask for his ideas in designing a method to integrate the enlightening thoughts into your life. Listen intently as William provides his sound advice. He will be a lifelong friend. You and this angel take in the view while leisurely strolling along the scenic pathway to peace.

Dosage: Once a day, or as desired.

Break Room

People evolve from a better understanding of their priorities in life. A powerful transformation develops when they become connected to an inner core essence. Visualize traveling to an area deep within the center of your body that holds your innermost self. Imagine the space as a quiet room in which to meditate and reflect. How does it look? Picture the décor and contents. Select a comfortable place to sit or lie down. Invite some favorite Angel Specialists to pay a visit to your room. Envision a peaceful future and create, in vivid detail, each aspect you desire. Add tangible and intangible items to bring you comfort. Embrace the sense of peace experienced. Come back to reality when leaving your room. As this sanctuary is within you, revisit it often.

Dosage: As desired, for peace of mind.

Color Me Balanced

The hallmark of a spiritual individual is the alignment of the mind, body, and spirit. Practicing the balancing remedy creates an overall sense of wholeness. Picture holding four bricks, each coated in one of these all-balancing colors: carnation pink (physical well-being), sky blue (emotional stability), yellow (mental clarity), and lavender (spiritual enlightenment). Imagine Ursula, Angel of Alignment, by a large green teeter-totter. The delicate and poised angel watches as you choose the seat to your left, placing a pink brick down first and then a blue one on top of it. Then put a yellow brick on the seat on your right, with a lavender one on top. Watch the teeter-totter level and come to balance. Ursula is in awe of your self-alignment.

Dosage: Every other day, or for balance.

To the Nines

Using the power of numbers can propel people to a higher level of spirituality. Every number has its own frequency. The numbers one through nine can be activated to elevate your own vibration. Begin this visualization by sitting comfortably in a chair. Bradley, Angel of Purpose, looks dashing, with his wavy dark hair and clear brown eyes. He seems delighted to be a part of this technique. Watch this angel take a laser-like beam and draw a number "1" directly down the center of your body. Feel the essence of this vibration with the warming sensation. After one minute, this light dissipates. Bradley draws the number "2" on your body. He continues the process with each number through "9." Afterward, the depth of your spirituality will have been extended immeasurably.

Dosage: Two nights a week, before bed.

Sparkling Spirit

Individuals experience a dramatic bounce in their step as they align with their angels. Call upon an angel for a terrific boost in energy. Paula, Angel of Energy, appears. She is holding a golden sparkling liquid in a long-stemmed glass. Bubbles of angelic blessings dance on the surface when she hands you a glass. Sip this sparkling, fizzy drink, enjoying a bright, effervescent energy. Envision the sparkles filling your body from head to toe. Golden sparkles pervade the air as everything lights up with a crystalline brightness. The light seen in Paula's eyes reflects a light in your heart that aligns you with the angels. Any time you want an extra boost of energy to supercharge your connection with the angels, Paula stops by and suggests one more powerful, "sparkling" drink. Its effervescence is invigorating.

Dosage: Twice a week, or for extra energy.

Serenity Float

Tranquil environments provide fertile ground for gathering advice. Notice Alicia, Angel of Serenity, who is wearing a lavender gown, a color signifying spirituality. She is lounging on a comfortable raft, also lavender, and floating down a placid river. Alicia has a raft for you. Climb aboard and push off. Floating side by side provides an opportunity to ask her for advice. Phrase all questions, "What do I need to know that I do not already know about _____?" Insert the subject of your query. Alicia's response is most helpful. Using this formula, continue to ask questions. Once all the answers have been obtained, thank the angel and head for shore. With Alicia's advice still in your mind, leave the raft at the bank. Now walk back at a quick pace.

Dosage: Twice a week, or for guidance.

Infinity for All

Universal energy is ever-present and readily available to harness as an unlimited source. Tapping into the permanent force allows for superb performance and superior enlightenment. To start, picture Archangel Uriel, Angel of Spirituality, with his gentle persona and heartwarming smile. The angel explains the technique. He bases it on the infinity symbol, a large figure eight drawn on its side. Begin by extending your dominant hand in front of you and making the movements of drawing a large infinity symbol. Archangel Uriel is drawing too. Repeat this same motion for at least seven rotations. Uriel watches as your energy gets a boost, putting you in supreme shape. Archangel Uriel states: "Universal energy is powerful. Tap into this resource."

Dosage: Throughout the day, for energy.

World of Love

Guardian Angels encourage love by using their unique talents for providing guidance based on superior knowledge. They share these specialties for the betterment of humanity and for this planet. With this remedy, you become connected to their expansive and angelic mission. Leslie, Angel of Diplomacy, wearing a brilliant blue gown with a gold ribbon, invites you to become a partner in this mission. See the gold ribbon leaving the waistband of her gown and floating up through the ceiling and out to the sky. The ribbon follows a vast circular path, traveling around the globe three times. The humans, animals, or other beings in the orbit of its golden radiant light have been blessed. Returning, it wraps around Leslie's waist again. She blesses you for your part in the mission.

Dosage: Every other day, in the evening.

Golden Temple

Spirituality, in which inner peace plays an integral role, supplies an untold number of blessings. Enliven spirituality with a meditation. To begin, light candles and have peaceful music in the background. Envision ascending a beautiful golden staircase leading to a golden temple. As you walk through two magnificent doors, observe some candles aglow throughout the room. The fragrance of roses fills the air. Catch the scent of jasmine incense as you are seated on a green velvet cushion. Josephine, Angel of Inner Peace, joins you. She has a gentle, soothing aura. Together you bask in the surroundings and meditate. Contemplate living in continual inner peace and embrace this feeling. Later, after descending the staircase, Josephine invites you to revisit the golden temple often.

Dosage: Once a day, for enlightened peace.

Preventive Medicine

Three remedies, three times a week
Four affirmations, two times a week

Prosperity Questions

Will Guardian Angels foster inner peace?
Angels encourage individuals to attain contentment and fulfillment in life, taking pride in supporting people on the search for the path to enlightenment. Through a connection to the divine, humans can experience harmony and universal love. Inner peace is the primary goal for those seeking true spirituality.

Angel Specialist: William, Angel of Peace

Primary Remedy: *Golden Temple*

Can angels help keep people in balance?
Individuals who interact with angels on a regular basis find it easy to maintain balance. Angelic assistance promotes a wholeness that keeps people centered. Personal and professional lives improve at a dramatic rate when angels intervene. Inner peace and harmony will be the ultimate result of this balance.

Angel Specialist: Robert, Angel of Balance

Primary Remedy: *To the Nines*

Second Opinion

Ruth Stout, LMT—*President: Heal-Thy Self Wellness Center with therapeutic massage or energy healing. Quantum-Touch Certified. Angelspeake Facilitator: Sessions and seminars.*

People who tap into their core of spirituality are able to experience prosperity and to live life in a truly harmonious state. A connection to the divine is one aspect of being spiritual. How individuals get to this point becomes a personal decision and is different for all those who choose this path. Spirituality requires some concentration and commitment. It means truly paying attention to the stillness within the soul. When individuals recognize their spiritual side, they make personal growth an intention. Enlightened people intuitively know the continual accessibility of this sought-after peace, which comes from within their internal belief system. Spirituality is the true path to inner peace and personal fulfillment.

Keywords: Spirituality. Enlightenment. Fulfillment.

Miracle Story

Chi for Two

Early one morning, in a sanctuary that was being used as a college hall, Christy was surprised to find that her Chi-Lel class had some unexpected visitors. The event is ingrained in her memory. Christy kept the story to herself for five years.

About fifteen individuals gathered together to practice a Chinese exercise for healing known as *Chi-Lel*. We met before daylight in a church sanctuary that had multiple stained-glass windows. These windows extended from floor to ceiling.

Our group was practicing in a circle, eyes closed. I heard a child giggling. I opened my eyes to see a chubby boy about four twirling in the circle. Practicing again, I was interrupted by two masculine voices on the side of the sanctuary. They commented on what we were doing so intently. One remark I heard was about the glow that was being generated within all of us from the high-level energy work. I became intrigued with the depth of the conversation.

Glancing in the direction of the voices, I saw some large angels sitting on the floor engaged in a discussion. As dawn broke and sunlight shone through the colorful stained-glass windows, all the magnificent angels faded away and the precious cherub vanished. I really believe that the angels came to the sanctuary to offer blessings to me and the others who were practicing the art of *Chi-Lel*.

This book is about relationships, happiness, and prosperity. The message from the angels to take with you after reading Angel First Aid *is: you are never alone and there is always hope. Look for synchronicity, because it will announce the close proximity of angels. When enjoying all the blessings from Guardian Angels, express gratitude and become open to receiving more. Invite angels into your life for continual love, happiness, and true prosperity.*

Glossary of Angels

Archangels

Gabriel, Angel of Communication: Delivers messages; works with the arts and inventions.

Michael, Angel of Protection: Offers insight, guidance, and direction; oversees divine justice.

Raphael, Angel of Healing: Creates strength and energy for well-being; promotes brotherhood.

Uriel, Angel of Spirituality: Promotes inner peace, prosperity, and enlightenment for mankind.

Angel Specialists

Alan, Angel of Investments: Nurtures financial growth; enhances sound fiscal decision-making.

Alexander, Angel of Invention: Inspires ideas; guides in design and development of prototypes.

Alicia, Angel of Serenity: Instills inner peace, harmony, and joy for genuine spirituality.

Allison, Angel of Plants: Supports cultivation initiatives and growth for different types of plants.

Annette, Angel of Gratitude: Encourages thankfulness through varied forms; offers appreciation.

Barbara, Angel of Fame: Assists in career development for aspiring entertainers and musicians.

Barry, Angel of Strength: Increases energy for stamina; provides strength, power, and support.

Bernard, Angel of Computers: Provides technical computer information; improves repair skills.

Bettina, Angel of Creativity: Inspires innovative visions to bolster the arts, science, and business.

Blake, Angel of Comfort: Promotes well-being through fulfillment, happiness, and contentment.

Bradley, Angel of Purpose: Assists in the search to identify a life's path; encourages motivation.

Brian, Angel of Relationships: Fosters harmonious and beneficial partnerships or associations.

Calvin, Angel of Real Estate: Guides a purchase or sale of residential or commercial properties.

Cameron, Angel of Weather: Protects during all storms; improves severe weather disturbances.

Caroline, Angel of Positive Thinking: Increases joyful, productive, and inspirational thoughts.

Christine, Angel of Spontaneity: Encourages instinctual impulses for achieving true happiness.

Christopher, Angel of Opportunity: Opens all doors to successful associations and prospects.

Constance, Angel of Public Relations: Generates media exposure; produces general publicity.

Cornell, Angel of Decisions: Evaluates pros and cons of pertinent information; offers choices.

Cory, Angel of Careers: Enhances skills or professional expertise; creates future opportunities.

Courtney, Angel of Responsibility: Organizes personal activities; accomplishes assigned duties.

Darla, Angel of Enlightenment: Inspires wisdom; offers insight, clarity of thought, and honesty.

Darrin, Angel of Housing: Helps to locate an affordable, adequate, and comfortable living space.

David, Angel of Camaraderie: Provides companionship and helps to build lifelong alliances.

Deborah, Angel of Interviewing: Bolsters professional interaction; increases self-confidence.

Denise, Angel of Accountants: Computes, performs, and analyzes numbers to manage finances.

Diane, Angel of Childcare: Endorses competent, reliable caregivers for nurturing and affection.

Douglas, Angel of Politics: Ensures credibility; fosters interactions with interested constituents.

Eileen, Angel of Happiness: Encourages well-being, joy, and delight; advocates true contentment.

Esther, Angel of Vitality: Generates stamina, energy, or liveliness for maintaining vibrant health.

Evelyn, Angel of Manifesting: Attracts each aspect of prosperity; wealth, success, and abundance.

Florence, Angel of Compassion: Generates pure feelings of kindness, empathy, or consideration.

Frances, Angel of Fertility: Provides positive interaction and blessings for conceiving children.

Francis, Angel of Wisdom: Offers a new perception and fresh connections for higher guidance.

George, Angel of Success: Assists in the development of goals; promotes professional careers.

Gordon, Angel of Focus: Boosts concentration for clear thinking; facilitates all comprehension.

Gunther, Angel of Fitness: Offers motivation for intense workouts; fortifies stamina, and endurance.

Hannah, Angel of Courage: Provides valor and encouragement, perseverance, and performance.

Harold, Angel of Support: Locates and supplies various mentors; offers comfort and security.

Irena, Angel of Patience: Improves ability to maintain a steady composure and to be centered.

Jacob, Angel of Education: Increases comprehension and focus; intensifies overall awareness.

James, Angel of Public Speaking: Bolsters confidence; improves the ability to convey messages.

Jason, Angel of Organization: Supplies order and focus; prioritizes and completes all projects.

Jennifer, Angel of Communication: Cultivates effective interaction and association amongst individuals.

Jeremiah, Angel of Financial Security: Creates wealth; increases funds for investing in assets.

Jessie, Angel of Deadlines: Arranges time to finish assignments, schoolwork, and projects.

Joanne, Angel of Relaxation: Encourages a serene environment to support recreational activities.

Jonathan, Angel of Business: Coordinates professional ventures to build financial success.

Jordan, Angel of Teamwork: Fosters camaraderie and joint efforts to achieve mutual objectives.

Joseph, Angel of Joy: Generates happiness; bestows contentment, joyfulness, and genuine bliss.

Josephine, Angel of Inner Peace: Promotes tranquility to ensure peace, serenity, and harmony.

Kathleen, Angel of Laughter: Encourages jovial release; promotes humor to increase happiness.

Katrina, Angel of Prosperity: Encourages abundance to foster happiness, wealth, and fulfillment.

Kevin, Angel of Friendship: Creates mutual affection to generate closeness, loyalty, and respect.

Kyle, Angel of Partnership: Enhances compatibility for mutually advantageous associations.

Laramie, Angel of Discovery: Provides assistance in the location of lost people, objects, and pets.

Lawrence, Angel of Endurance: Encourages strength, stamina, and resilience; boosts personal power.

Leslie, Angel of Diplomacy: Advocates peacekeeping for successful mediations and negotiations.

Lois, Angel of Clarity: Sharpens concentration; stimulates the mind for better insight or wisdom.

Lorena, Angel of Divine Grace: Distributes a wealth of blessings for enriching all aspects of life.

Loretta, Angel of New Enterprise: Facilitates endeavors associated with new business ventures.

Lucian, Angel of Resources: Creates novel opportunities to receive wealth, prosperity, and joy.

Madeline, Angel of Teachers: Oversees learning formats; improves ability to impart knowledge.

Marcus, Angel of Sales: Perfects super selling techniques to assure more profitable transactions.

Mariann, Angel of Efficiency: Bolsters real effectiveness to sharpen focus and advance abilities.

Marilyn, Angel of Leisure: Bestows numerous resources for relaxation, including fun vacations.

Mary Jo, Angel of Print Media: Inspires absolute creativity for very successful journalistic efforts.

Maureen, Angel of Time: Assists in managing time with punctuality; helps meet tight deadlines.

Melody, Angel of Self-Esteem: Maintains internal belief in personal value and true confidence.

Melvin, Angel of TV: Increases creative ideas for design, content, production, and programming.

Michelle, Angel of Radio Hosts: Encourages connection and interaction with a diverse audience.

Mirra, Angel of Healing Arts: Sustains all modalities for healing; helps healthcare practitioners.

Nancy, Angel of Productivity: Initiates performance and efficiency for varied projects and tasks.

Natalie, Angel of Contentment: Generates satisfaction, or provides resources for everlasting joy.

Nicole, Angel of Negotiation: Leads mutually successful mediation to secure solid transactions.

Pamela, Angel of Environment: Encourages optimal life conditions for humans and the planet.

Patrick, Angel of Sports: Coaches athletes for increased proficiency and excellent performance.

Paula, Angel of Energy: Improves strength and power to add essential vitality, pep, and stamina.

Perrie, Angel of Music: Enhances talents through encouraging unique musical expression.

Peter, Angel of Health: Cultivates wholeness, well-being, and dynamic energy; optimizes health.

Phillip, Angel of Employment: Promotes job-related situations to advance professional endeavors.

Rachel, Angel of Inspiration: Delivers messages to motivate creative thoughts and upbeat ideas.

Randolph, Angel of Expansion: Arranges more chances for optimal success, personal and career.

Raymond, Angel of Technology: Oversees operation of all machines; supports electronic devices.

Rebecca, Angel of Confidence: Bolsters and strengthens self-esteem for additional self-reliance.

Rex, Angel of Cars: Works with mechanics; orchestrates dependable automotive performance.

Rita, Angel of Writing: Clarifies original thoughts; promotes the expression of true creativity.

Robert, Angel of Balance: Helps achieve equilibrium or stability for centering and grounding.

Robin, Angel of Social Contact: Organizes events, dates, and parties for friends and associates.

Ruth, Angel of Divine Justice: Settles disputes; assures fair decisions for equitable resolutions.

Sally, Angel of Perseverance: Bolsters determination or persistence to design and attain goals.

Samuel, Angel of Excellence: Enhances desire to attain a high level of performance in all arenas.

Sarah, Angel of Harmony: Promotes caring, balanced, or tranquil interaction; encourages peace.

Serena, Angel of Children: Nurtures, loves, and protects youngsters; plus those young at heart.

Sherrill, Angel of Stability: Promotes solid foundation to balance individuals or circumstances.

Solomon, Angel of Security: Supplies emotional stability, safety, and a true sense of well-being.

Susan, Angel of Travel: Sparks the desire for adventure; protects throughout trips or journeys.

Tara, Angel of Love: Distributes blessings of unconditional love, nurturing, and genuine acceptance.

Terina, Angel of Attraction: Endorses true compatibility; finds soulmates; intersects their paths.

Theodore, Angel of Kindness: Offers affection, devotion, and compassion; nurtures relationships.

Theresa, Angel of Empowerment: Strengthens personal power; bolsters genuine self-confidence.

Thomas, Angel of Animal Care: Orchestrates healing, love, and protection for pets and animals.

Timothy, Angel of Good Fortune: Offers financial gain, wealth, abundance, and true prosperity.

Trevor, Angel of Stocks: Guides market evaluations; supports investments for successful endeavors.

Tully, Angel of Invention: Develops products for the creation of unique, innovative devices.

Tyler, Angel of Abundance: Supplies generous amounts of prosperity, affluence, and happiness.

Ursula, Angel of Alignment: Creates a state of balance, so energies are in sync for optimal flow.

Valerie, Angel of Understanding: Increases tolerance and awareness; improves comprehension.

Victoria, Angel of Guidance: Provides advice or direction; conveys timely, pertinent information.

Walter, Angel of Banking: Supervises banking procedures and transactions to increase net worth.

Wayne, Angel of Publishing: Ensures solid connections amongst authors, editors, or publishers.

William, Angel of Peace: Offers harmony and tranquility; fosters greater unity amongst nations.

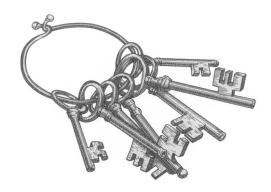

Keys to Prosperity

This index is a list of remedies that can be referenced by a keyword. Consider the desired outcome you would like to achieve. Look up a keyword that best describes the situation, circumstance, or solution. Select the remedy for preferred results.

* *Best remedy to use*

* *Best remedy to use*

Best remedy to use

Best remedy to use

* Best remedy to use

* *Best remedy to use*

* Best remedy to use

* Best remedy to use

* Best remedy to use

* Best remedy to use

* *Best remedy to use*

* *Best remedy to use*

* Best remedy to use

Contacting The Angel Lady

Calls for consultations, speaking engagements,
and interviews are always welcome.

Angelight Productions

800-323-1790

630-420-1334

630-420-1474 (Fax)

theangellady@comcast.net

www.theangellady.net

When sending e-mail,
please include phone number